Around the World

A Postcard Adventure

Pamela Terry

ⱺuest press • Los Angeles

Around the World: A Postcard Adventure is a true story. Most of the names have been changed to protect the privacy of friends, and those I met along my journey.

P.T.

Published by Quest Press

Around the World: A Postcard Adventure Copyright ©1996 by Pamela R. Terry
All rights reserved under International and Pan-American Copyright Conventions.

Cover Design Copyright © 1996 *by Susan Lavoie*

Publisher's Cataloging in Publication
(Prepared by Quality Books Inc.)

Terry, Pamela, 1961-
Around the world : a postcard adventure / Pamela Terry.
p. cm.
ISBN 0-9648555-9-3
Preassigned LCCN: 95-71166

1. Voyages around the world. 2. Terry, Pamela, 1961- --
Journeys. I. Title.

G440.T47 1995   910.4'1
QBI95-20477

Printed in Singapore

To my mother, Joan D. Terry,
who suggested the trip in the first place.

ROAD MAP

1. Los Angeles, California U.S.A.

2. Tokyo, Japan

3. Taipei, Taiwan

4. Hong Kong

5. Canton, China

6. Singapore

7. Bombay, India

8. Navsari, India

9. Vienna, Austria

10. Venice, Italy

11. Florence, Italy

12. Frankfurt, Germany

13. Hamburg, Germany

14. Berlin, Germany

15. Zurich, Switzerland

16. Paris, France

17. Atlanta, Georgia, U.S.A., and back to Los Angeles, California

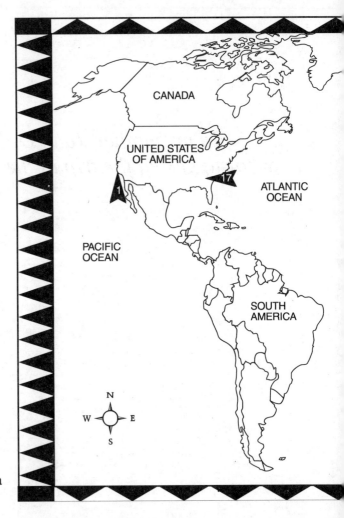

THE ROUTE

Dear Traveler,

I always wanted to be a traveler, but it wasn't until I bought a *Round The World* airline ticket and a Eurailpass for the European trains for a 2 month global trip that I actually felt like a traveler.

I planned my trip very carefully to see as much as I possibly could in each city I visited. I had only two rules: #1 – I was not going to sleep in any hostels, clean hotels were a must. #2 – All hotels must have USA accepted toilet facilities, no squatters-right hole in the floor for this USA born and bred woman.

Traveling on a budget of $80 a day for lodging, food, transportation, souvenirs, post-cards and stamps, I embarked on this voyage.

During my journey I sent myself postcards home detailing my adventures, and it is the events on those postcards that are featured in this book.

The postcards were written on the road, during the rush of being on the road, not in retrospect and reflection after the trip was over. There has been as little editing as possible to preserve the original emotions and intent. The postcards cover the full sweep of my experiences, including surprises, frustrations, fears, tears, disasters and triumphs, from traveling companion mishaps, to a bus accident in India, to conversations with the locals in a pub in Vienna.

I am not the type of person to keep up with writing a travel diary, but I can write a postcard in a minute. I looked upon it as a challenge to get the postcards written and mailed while I was still in the country. Not to be left unmentioned, I am ultimately cheap. If I spent the money on the stamps when I purchased the postcards, I knew I was going to get the postcards mailed.

Before my trip I thought I knew how to travel, but the knowledge I constantly gained led me to start my trip with two suitcases and finish it with one.

In the end no matter how much planning I did prior to my trip the constant unexpected adventures that occurred in every city are what ultimately made it a magnificent journey.

I hope you enjoy the trip as much as I did.

Bon Voyage
Pam

There go those feet again

LOS ANGELES AIRPORT TO TOKYO, JAPAN - 2 January

It's so exciting to fly out of the international terminal at LAX. The only other time I flew overseas I was on a US carrier, so I left out of the regular domestic terminal. This time I'm taking Singapore Airlines so I can be an international traveler.

I have a travel companion, Diane, for the Asia part of my trip. We're going to the same wedding in India, so she asked to join me on my other Asia stops. It will be nice to have someone to split the cost of the hotels. I hope we get along.

Love, Pam

TOKYO, JAPAN - 3 January

Diane and I arrived in Tokyo, as the sun was setting. There was a plane at our gate, I think they said Singapore only has one gate at Narita Airport, so we had to wait to deplane. It seemed like forever after the 12 hour flight.

We cleared customs easily and found the airport bus limo booth. The man was kind enough to write down the name of our hotel, "The Asia Center of Japan," in Japanese for us.

It's a 41 mile drive to downtown Tokyo and the bus only cost *$20US*, a taxi would have cost *$150US*. The bus ride took two hours. I, semi-slept along the way. We caught the bus to the Akasaka Tokyo Hotel, then took a taxi to our cheap hotel, "The Asia Center of Japan," for *$5US*.

When we got to Tokyo, I was suprised, everything was closed, at 10:30 in the evening?

Love, Pam

TOKYO, JAPAN - 4 January

The Diet building is the Japan Parliament building, I saw it through big iron gates on my Grey Line tour. We were not allowed inside or even on the grounds. It is one of the older buildings in Tokyo. It was closed for the New Year. After visiting the Diet building, we headed for the Meiji Shrine. The grounds are huge.

1,000,000 people were there. They sold souvenirs to the worshipers. I felt uncomfortable being on a tour in the Shrine on a holy day.

Love, Pam

TOKYO, JAPAN - 4 January

Tokyo is a very expensive city. We have looked around for cheap Japanese tea. The cost of a cup of tea has ranged from *$7.00US* to *$11.00US*. The dollar is doing better the longer we're here, but Diane wants to get started so early each day, that we lose out on the better exchange rate. The early departure gets us to our destination while it's still closed.

Love, Pam

TOKYO, JAPAN - 5 January

Tokyo is not a very beautiful city, but it is very clean. Life seems to center around working and shopping. The Japanese love to shop, and they will wait in line for hours for sales. When we got off the subway, having been directed to an area for Diane to shop, we saw masses of people waiting to get into a department store. The lines went all around the building and even into the subway station, kind of like an after Christmas sale in America.

I was here at a very special time of year. Although many shops were closed, many women wore kimonos, which the tour guide said only happens during the New Year.

Love, Pam

TOKYO, JAPAN - 5 January

I'm so tired. My cold weakened me a lot before I left. Also, my feet hurt. So what else is new? The moment I step off the North American continent my feet hurt. *My feet never give me problems at home, but they always give me problems when I take a trip.*

The people have been very nice and very helpful. We always got our destination written in Japanese, and people do their best to help us. They don't speak English, but they point. The first day, two men walked us to the subway and helped us with the tickets. I would never have known which Japanese symbol to push or what coin to put in the machine.

Love, Pam

TOKYO, JAPAN - 5 January

The feet saga starts once again. My feet were damp after my shower. I dried them as best I could, but they were still damp, so I put baby powder on them. Big mistake.

The powder built up a friction on my feet causing them to rub against my socks and burn. I hobbled back to the Asia Center of Japan. Grateful the subway station had two escalators so my feet could rest.

Love, Pam

TOKYO, JAPAN - 5 January

The women in Tokyo wore beautiful shawls and I wanted to get my sister, Kim, one, but they were too expensive. All the men seemed to wear the same navy blue suit.

Diane and I went to a seaweed shop today. It's kind of like a coffee and tea shop in the United States, but they sell seaweed. She bought a can because she thought she couldn't leave without buying something, after the man had spent a lot of time with her. I was given a free cup of tea while Diane shopped for seaweed. I wound up spilling it on myself. So much for the graceful American.

Love, Pam

TOKYO, JAPAN - 5 January

After we left the seaweed shop I had to go to the bathroom, really bad. Everything was closed. My only hope was to get into the Mitsukoshi department store. We walked to the head of the line. You could feel the people seething behind us after all the hours they'd waited. I knocked on the glass door as a saleswoman rushed by. She came to the door trying to tell me to get in line. I explained my problem to her, promising to leave the store before it opened. She let us in. The crowd immediately reacted. She quickly gave us directions to the bathroom as she ran outside to calm the crowd. I felt like all of Tokyo suddenly knew I had to pee.

See Card #2

Love, Pam

TOKYO, JAPAN - 5 January

CARD #2

We found the bathroom quickly. I was grateful to see a stall with a *W* on the door. *W* stands for Western, meaning standard American toilet. I went in there. All the other stalls had Eastern toilets.

Eastern toilets are shaped like a bassinet with the hood up on one end, seated on the floor. I was sent a brochure from the Japan National Tourist Organization, JNTO, with illustrations on how to properly use an Eastern toilet. To use one, you face the hooded area, straddle the sides of the bassinet, and squat down, flushing afterwards.

Whenever I opened a stall with an Eastern toilet, I held it. I've had back and knee problems, and was not about to be embarrassed by falling into the toilet.

Love, Pam

TOKYO, JAPAN - 5 January

After receiving the toilet brochure I asked every hotel I called about the toilets before making a reservation. When one hotel said they'd show me how to use the toilet, I knew it wasn't the hotel for me.

Diane apparently hadn't read the JNTO toilet literature. When she told me she held onto the flusher to help keep her balance I thought, wow! she has some reach. From that position the flusher is over a yard away.

At some point she saw a pictograph and realized she was using the toilet backwards. She had held on to the flusher directly behind her.

Love, Pam

TOKYO, JAPAN - 5 January

Dear Kim:

The people in Tokyo love to shop. But there are no bargains anywhere. Diane likes to shop, but you know it drives me crazy, quickly. She wanted to buy a pair of socks like the women wear with kimonos. They don't go between the big toe but between the toe next to the big toe. The Japanese women wear cotton socks, but polyester socks are made for bigger feet. Diane was upset because she needed the polyester size. They really weren't as attractive as the cotton ones, so she didn't buy them.

I took a Grey Line tour, it showed the major sites. Lots of things were closed for the New Year.

Love, Pam

TOKYO, JAPAN - 6 January

NARITA AIRPORT:

Diane got tired from all the walking at the airport. Her carry on is too heavy, but mostly, she didn't know when all the checks were going to stop. Security, X-Ray, Checked Baggage, Ticket Counter, Exit Ticket Counter, Exit Tax Collection, Passport Control, Immigration, Carry On X-Ray Counter, it didn't bother me, it all just seemed so international. I loved it all.

Also, my passport keeps getting more stamps in it. Unlike my European Tour trip with only one stamp.

Love, Pam

TOKYO, JAPAN - 6 January

NARITA AIRPORT:

I really surprised this one Indian man who worked at the airport. On Singapore Airlines the 747 business and first class passengers get on down a separate companion way than coach. I was wearing my red shirt and sweat pants, and I had my daypack on. He stopped me and asked to see my boarding pass. I turned it towards him and he saw my business class blue boarding pass. He didn't know what to say to this big woman. I just smiled.

Love, Pam

2

You! Get out
of the cab!

TAIPEI, TAIWAN - 6 January

We arrived in Taipei, 30 minutes late, it was drizzling. We quickly got our luggage then caught a loud, rickety, bus, 34 kilometers into town.

We arrived on a Sunday but I had forgotten about that until it was time to board the bus, so by the time we got into Taipei, we had very little money.

The bus let us off, it said, in front of the railway station, but all I could see were fruit stands and a very busy street.

A man on the bus said the YMCA was in back of the Hilton. The Hilton was on the opposite side of the street. Reachable only by going up a very long flight of stairs, leading to a bridge, crossing the bridge, and going down another very long set of stairs. It was impossible to cross on street level because subway construction had the street torn up.

After navigating our luggage through the fruit and tourist stands, we got to the bottom of the steps. I watched Diane heave her suitcase up three of the steps with all her strength. I knew it was time for a new plan.
See Card #2

Love, Pam

TAIPEI, TAIWAN - 6 January

CARD #2

Diane didn't want to spend the money on a taxi so she started going towards the bridge with her suitcase. The streets were full of vendors and pedestrians, so getting through was no easy task. My suitcases almost tumbled off the cart, twice. I hit a mannequin and almost knocked it down. Then, some locals helped me get my suitcases down the curb. When I finally got to the bridge I looked at what seemed to be a never ending staircase, and said "no way." I decided to hail a cab.
See Card #3

Love, Pam

TAIPEI, TAIWAN - 6 January

CARD #3

There were a bunch of taxis driving by so I flagged one. He lifted Diane's suitcase and his eyes bulged out because it's so heavy. Once the luggage was in the taxi we got in and said YMCA. I didn't expect him to speak English but major places I did expect a taxi driver to recognize. He didn't. Diane took out our hotel list and showed him. I didn't expect the man to read English, I don't know why she did. Surprisingly, he started driving.
See Card #4

Love, Pam

TAIPEI, TAIWAN - 6 January

CARD #4

I thought the taxi driver had realized that the YMCA was just across the street, but when he went several blocks without making a turn I knew he was about to take us for a ride. Suddenly near an underpass, he pulled the taxi over, took some change from his dash pointed at Diane, shouting, "You get out of the cab." That scared Diane to death. She panicked, screaming, "I'm not getting out by myself." I hurried out of the cab with her. I thought he was going to remove

our things from the cab because the YMCA wasn't a far enough fare.
See Card #5

Love, Pam

TAIPEI, TAIWAN - 6 January

CARD #5

There we were standing in the rain, in the middle of Taipei rush hour, with no idea what was happening. Next, the taxi driver went to the pay phone, I went with him. He dialed then gave me the phone. It was tourist information. I told the man on the phone that I wanted to go to the YMCA. Then he had me give the phone back to the taxi dirver. He gave the taxi driver the YMCA phone number. The driver called, got directions, and took us.

The bellman at the YMCA met us outside and told us to give the driver a big tip, twice the amount, *80¢US.* I couldn't believe it, bellman at the YMCA? Final Card.

Love, Pam

TAIPEI, TAIWAN - 7 January

We took a city tour today. There were only four people in the van, Diane and I, a Swiss man and a Chinese man. We went to the Martyr Shrine. Taiwan's equivalent to the US Tomb of the Unknown Soldier. We arrived just in time for the changing of the guards. It's the first time I'd ever seen a bayonet up close. They could certainly kill someone. The tallest soldiers in the Taiwan Army are the guards at the Martyr's Shrine. There are not many tall Taiwanese men, even the guards have to stand on concrete pedestals.

We went to a Taoist Temple. Outside old men sat in chairs, smoking. Inside it had stacks of stuff, books, figurines, just stuff all over the place in no obvious order. To me, it looked like a junky thrift store with Catholic incense.

Love, Pam

TAIPEI, TAIWAN - 7 January

Food in Taipei is very expensive. Toast and a glass of juice costs *$5.50US*. For lunch, I broke down and ate at Kentucky Fried Chicken; I took a photo there, you'll see it. I got a complete meal for *$3.50US*. They had soda I could drink without ice, so I enjoyed an iodine free drink. You have to always be on your guard with the food you eat and what you drink so you don't get sick. I've been putting Iodine drops in everything I drink to avoid stomach problems from bacteria in unfamiliar water, that includes ice cubes.

Love, Pam

TAIPEI, TAIWAN - 7 January

There are a lot of people in Taipei. I was surprised when Diane said it was more crowded here than in India. I find that hard to believe, but I'll know in a week. She's been to India before for another wedding, so she may be right.

Taipei gets most of its rain in January. Today didn't disappoint. I put on my new raincoat and went out for several hours browsing among the shopping stalls. I came back completely drenched. I'll call the catalogue lady in New York, who sold me the raincoat, to complain when I get home.

Love, Pam

TAIPEI, TAIWAN - 7 January

Dear Kim:

I took a tour of Taipei today. It was better than the Tokyo tour. The van could get into more places than the big tour bus. Afterwards we went looking in the shopping stalls. I bought a necklace for $8.31US. we've had a lot of adventures in Taiwan. Diane constantly worries about getting rid of her money. even when I told her she could change it back to US dollars at the airport. The Taiwan government doesn't want their money to leave its country.

Walking in the rain. I kind of hurt my knee. It'll be okay.

Love. Pam

TAIPEI. TAIWAN - 7 January

Dear Mom and Dad:

I'm sitting here in the YMCA. It's a very nice hotel with a nice staff. It's 11:00pm and I'm writing postcards in the lobby. before we leave for Hong Kong tomorrow. People do not speak English in Taipei. making for many escapades here. I'm sure you've read the other postcards.

Diane can be very trying and I miss all of you very much. I hope all is well.

My best to all.

Love. Pam

TAIPEI, TAIWAN - 7 January

I understand now why some people who intend to travel together go their separate ways after a short period of time. I have never spent so much time with someone who's so anal retentive. Diane won't even walk to the corner alone, or even to the front desk. If I say I'm not going to buy a soda, then she won't. The girl needs help.

Love, Pam

TAIPEI, TAIWAN - 7 January

If Diane repacks her suitcase one more time, I think I'll scream. She is constantly trying to make me pack travel books she wanted to bring. I refuse. She walks behind me on busy streets so I'll almost get hit by the cars, instead of her.

She can't make a single decision on her own, and she's always going to the bathroom because she's nervous. Ahhhhhhh!

Love, Pam

TAIPEI, TAIWAN - 7 January

Diane is so cheap that all she packed were samples for the trip. That would be okay, except she packed only 12 tampons, regular, and she normally uses super, so she's taking all the pads from the toilet on the plane. When we passed a drug store and a convenience store, but she didn't stop to buy any. She's just waiting for the plane to Hong Kong tomorrow.

I gave her a couple of pads, but I packed just enough for me. She'll have to solve her own problems.

Love, Pam

TAIPEI, TAIWAN - 8 January

Departure taxes can really mess up a budget. I bought a necklace yesterday, leaving me with only *$8.00US* for dinner and breakfast. I skipped dinner and had Dim Sum for breakfast, but it was too sweet. I also had funky tasting orange juice. It was only *$1.50US*, total.

We always set the departure tax money aside the very first thing when we enter a country so we know we can get out. Tokyo has a *$20.00US* departure tax. In Taiwan, it's *$11.29US* departure tax. Hong Kong has a *$15.00US* departure tax.

In the US we let you out for free.

Love, Pam

I have subsequently learned that we don't let you out for free. It's part of the ticket price if you purchase your ticket in the US or on a US carrier abroad.

New Territories

HONG KONG

Kowloon

Hong Kong
Island

SOUTH CHINA SEA

3

The anal retentive traveling companion

HONG KONG - 8 January

After breakfast in Taipei, consisting of a small and medium Dim Sum and a lousy orange juice, that was made in the USA, I was very hungry by our 3:00pm flight, from Taipei to Hong Kong.

Singapore Airlines served what they called a "light meal," but it was a feast to me. Poached salmon, lobster salad, carrots, broccoli, rolls, water, juice, chocolate grinosh, coffee. I didn't eat dinner this night, neither did Diane. She's always afraid to venture out alone.

The view from the plane coming into Hong Kong was beautiful. The plane came in low over the clear blue waters of Hong Kong harbor. The white high-rises on the shore seemed so cosmopolitan. The runway jets out right into the center of the harbor. I asked for a window seat specifically for this view. My friend, Sheila, told me how great this landing was. She was right.

When we arrived in Hong Kong, we took a cab from the airport. The driver cheated us, a little, by charging us $40.00 Hong Kong instead of $37.70 Hong Kong. Either way, it was only *$5.50US* total. *$2.25US* for door to door service, sounds good to me.

Love, Pam

HONG KONG - 8 January

When we arrived in Hong Kong we of course got the only taxi driver at the airport who spoke no English, and I'd forgotten to get YMCA written in Chinese. I thought it was going to be Taiwan all over again, but he recognized the words Star Ferry and took us to the YMCA we wanted.

We are on the Kowloon side of Hong Kong, which is where the Hong Kong Airport is really located. It's kind of confusing unless you think of Kowloon and Hong Kong like twin cities, Minneapolis/St. Paul or Dallas/Fort Worth.

I walked along Nathan road at night. It was crazy. Lots of snakes, touts, and con men are everywhere, trying to sell their wares. It was the first time I physically had my hand on my belt bag when I walked. The crowds never let up.

Love, Pam

HONG KONG - 8 January

Once in Hong Kong my most immediate concern was to find a laundromat. The desk clerk at the YMCA said to try the Chungking Mansion. This intrigued me because I wanted to see the infamous Chungking Mansion. It's not a mansion, at least not from the entrance elevator, which is in a shopping arcade where a lot of snake business men hang out trying to get you take their cards. It looked so seedy that I didn't even enter the elevator. I thought I'd get diseased just by pushing the button.

I did make the mistake of taking one business card, because then they were all after me.

Love, Pam

HONG KONG - 8 January

After returning to the YMCA with my dirty laundry, I decided to put that off for awhile. Instead I scoured through all the brochures and throwaway tourist newspapers I could find, looking for the best deal on custom tailored clothing. I knew it took more than the 24 hours it use to take years ago, but we had just enough time to choose the material, pattern and get a fitting before we left Hong Kong. They could mail the clothes home to us.

See Card #2

Love, Pam

HONG KONG - 9 January

CARD #2

I found a great deal on a tailor, I located his shop on the map and it was within walking distance. We left the YMCA early, but for once not too early, Diane, our dirty laundry, and me.

We found the tailor and chose material. Diane selected a beautiful aqua with a soft embossment. She is having them duplicate a dress she likes of her grandmother's. It's a form fitting simple short dress that will look very attractive on her. She was smart and brought the actual dress with her. The cutter took the dress so he could make an exact pattern from it.

See Card #3

Love, Pam

HONG KONG - 9 January

CARD #3

The tailor didn't have a large choice of fabrics for women's clothes. Diane probably selected the prettiest piece in the store. I selected a black silk print for a dress, and a solid black silk for a jacket. The dress material is OK, but the silk jacket is wonderful. It's jet black, and it feels like liquid mercury as it runs through your fingers. I'm going to like wearing that jacket!

Love, Pam

HONG KONG - 9 January

Good News! The tailor told us where to find a laundry. It was in a narrow corridor just across the street from them. We would have never found it on our own. The counter clerk stressed "Do not lose your ticket," as we gave him our clothes. If we lose the ticket there is a big additional charge. I'm not going to lose that ticket.

Love, Pam

HONG KONG - 9 January

Hong Kong is crowded, but not as crowded as Taipei. When you walk down the streets in Hong Kong you feel you are being hustled. In Taipei, you felt these people are poor, and they're trying to make a living selling everything from clothes, to hot food, to chewing gum.

The YMCA in Hong Kong is very centrally located, near the Star Ferry and Nathan road. Nathan Road has lots of shops.

Mom, I got my camera battery, for half price just as you said. I only had to bargain at three camera stores, but they were right next door to each other on Nathan Road.

Love, Pam

HONG KONG - 9 January

Diane has a list of a few things she wants to buy on this trip. The kimono socks were a bust in Tokyo, so here in Hong Kong she wants to buy a rosewood jewelry box. After the tailor's, we went to several stores looking at rosewood boxes, but she couldn't decide. She thinks she will get a better bargain at some other unknown store. I'm staying patient and not getting angry. Yet.

Love, Pam

HONG KONG - 9 January

UNUSUAL SIGHTINGS

It's a weird thing, in Hong Kong and Taipei, the display cases in the stores all have a small glass of water in them, tucked away in the corner. It's about the size of a shot glass. I don't know if the water is for the humidity, maybe the windows would fog over otherwise. I've tried to find out the answer but every time I ask someone about it they don't speak English.

Love, Pam

HONG KONG - 9 January

We took the ferry across the harbor to Hong Kong. I took the advice of the Fielding's "Budget Asia" book and sat downstairs with the locals. It is cheaper that way. It was windy but the ferry ride was very fast. I saw a post office on the dock from the ferry. In our quest to find it we passed by the area where the homeless people live in cardboard boxes. Of course Diane would pick this spot, the only time on the whole trip, to stop and re-tie her shoes.

Love, Pam

HONG KONG - 9 January

When I got off the ferry on the Hong Kong side, we saw some rickshaw drivers. I reached to take out my camera and two came running up. An old man beat the young man. He insisted that I get in the rickshaw. I tried to say no, but he insisted. So I got in and Diane took my picture. After that, he tried to charge me $100.00 Hong Kong, *$13.30US*. I told him no, that he came to me. He tried to charge me more because I'm large. I gave him $70.00 Hong Kong, *$10.00US*, waved my hand hard and walked away.

Love, Pam

HONG KONG - 9 January

I took the ferry across to Hong Kong because I wanted to get to Stanley Market. I had heard it's a place one could find good deals. I took a look at the map
after I got off the rickshaw and realized that it was on the opposite side of the island, so I got a bus.

For the first time on the whole trip, I was on a regular public bus. The view was breathtaking on the route up to Stanley Market. We were above the Hong Kong coast line, and the road was windy and narrow, but the coastal expanse was spectacular.

Love, Pam

HONG KONG - 9 January

Stanley Market is at the end of the bus line, after our windy coastal drive. It's said the locals shop here, which might be true. A few fishermen have their boats nearby. They have good prices and I bought a few things. The merchants say the prices are fixed, but if you go up to them quietly and make an offer they do bargain.

I bargained for a scarf, but later saw it on another stall for about 40% less. That's OK, it didn't cost much. But I do like a bargain. C'est la vie.

Love, Pam

CHINA

Canton
(Guangzhou)

Shekou

Hong
Kong

SOUTH CHINA SEA

N
W ◆ E
S

4

When they said, 'Giant Panda,' I thought they meant GIANT Panda

BOAT TO SHEKOU. CHINA – 10 January

Hi Daddy,

I promised you I'd write you from China. Actually this is on the boat, a very choppy ride, going to China. It's an hour long boat ride, after which we see the Terra Cotta Warriors, and take a two hour bus ride. It sounds as if it's going to be a good tour. Wish you were here.

I love you.

Pam

SHENCHEN, CHINA - 10 January

FIRST STOP:

I finally made it to Mainland China, my first communist country. I was excited at the opportunity to see some of the Terra Cotta Warrior statues after seeing pictures of the battalions of them. I had wanted to see reams and reams of soldiers but the museum in Shenchen only had three and a horse on display. The remainder are at the actual find. A two hour plane ride away in Xi'an. These were still worth seeing. No pictures are allowed, too bad.

Love, Pam

SHENCHEN, CHINA - 10 January

After the Terra Cotta Warriors we were taken to a kindergarten in Shenchen. Shenchen is in an Economic Development Zone. I think it's almost a small experiment in capitalism.

The children at the kindergarten performed a dance for us using colorful fans. They were very cute. After the fan dance, the teacher put on western music and the kids pulled people from the tour group onto the dance floor to dance with them. It was all very charming.

Love, Pam

SHENCHEN, CHINA - 10 January

The tour took us to a food market in Shenchen. On the outside it looks like an eight story apartment building, but on the bottom floor at least it's a market. I was surprised to see an abundance of fresh vegetables. There were tomatoes, carrots, potatoes, scallions, and lots more. Most of the books I've read about China, told about the lack of vegetables and the poor quality. These looked of good quality to me. Although the vendors smoking directly over the vegetables wasn't very appealing.

Love, Pam

SHENCHEN, CHINA - 10 January

On my way out of the market I saw a table of chickens. Fortunately they were already dead, plucked, and cleaned. I don't know why I thought they'd be in a pen where a customer would pick one and have the head cut off on the spot. It was unusual to see cleaned chickens that still had their feet. Their little claws were sticking up in the air from the table.

Love, Pam

SHENCHEN, CHINA - 10 January

Shenchen is a town with a very young population. The average age is only 32 years old. I think it's some sort of social experiment. That may be the reason for the good food at the market. At least the kids are happy.

Love, Pam

SOMEWHERE IN SOUTHERN CHINA - 10 January

Dear Dad,

The Terra Cotta Warrior statues are amazing! They were found by farmers in 1974. They were made 2,000 years ago for the tomb of the First Emperor, and buried underground for safe keeping and forgotten about. They only had a few on display. I'm on the run.

Love, Pam

SOMEWHERE IN SOUTHERN CHINA - 10 January

The two hour bus ride through southern China turned into eight hours, including lunch. Mostly, we saw poor people dressed in gray sitting around with piles of trash everywhere. The bus did stop for the obligatory pictures of the ducks. It's promised in the brochure. Most of the roads were dirt except for a five mile stretch of highway they were building.

Love, Pam

CANTON, CHINA - 10 January

Our last stop on the tour was the Canton zoo. The animals didn't look much happier than they do in most zoos. The main event was supposed to be the Giant Pandas. I was expecting great big bears, really GIANT pandas, but they looked small to me. I couldn't get over how small they were. They were about the size of one of those big stuffed pandas you get at a carnival.

Love, Pam

CANTON, CHINA - 10 January

The people in China were not very kind to me. They laughed at me constantly. They are never exposed to anyone from outside their culture, so this is the way they reacted.

I was very surprised at the living conditions. It's a dirty third world country, trash is piled up everywhere. I have no desire to go back. They did serve a tasty lunch at a restaurant somewhere in Southern China. The tour guide didn't want to tell me that the fish served was carp, because many people consider it bait.

Love, Pam

P.S. Even in the large city of Canton I didn't see any foreigners on the streets.

CHINA, GOING TO HONG KONG - 10 January

We took the train back to Hong Kong from China. They had a cheap boxed dinner, of chicken and rolls, you could buy on the train. The chicken was sopping in grease without much meat. I preferred the carp served at lunch. Now I understand why all the people on the tour who had heard about the food beforehand, brought their own food from Hong Kong.

Love, Pam

CHINA, GOING TO HONG KONG - 10 January

The Hong Kong government has specific rules about using the bathroom on the Chinese train. When you exit China and cross the boarder into Hong Kong's New Territory, you can no longer use the bathrooms. I think they lock them. So plan ahead accordingly.

Love, Pam

HONG KONG - 11 January

I packed last night but I got up early because some of my clothes were at a laundry. When we got back from China last night it was too late to pick them up. Diane, always anal about being late, put up such a nervous fit that we once again left the YMCA early.

We found a market and bought snacks. The store she wanted to look for which sold rosewood boxes, was closed until 10:00am, and it was 8:45am. So we picked up the laundry, and paid $75.00 Hong Kong, *$3.00US,* for everything I had packed. Then we had to wait for an hour for the tailor to open for her to get her final fitting. I had offered her the option of staying longer at the hotel, but she would not hear of it. She is difficult!

Love, Pam

HONG KONG - 11 January

Diane has an inability to make a decision. She constantly wonders if she can get a better deal somewhere else. That would be all right if she were willing to return to whatever place she wanted to buy it herself, but she won't do anything alone. We became separated at Stanley Market, which is not a very big bazarr, and I kept looking while she got upset that she couldn't find me and she had to stop shopping. The girl needs a shrink.

Love, Pam

HONG KONG - 11 January

Diane liked the Hong Kong YMCA best, of all the places we've stayed. The YMCA representative in the lobby gave me the creeps. Although the beds were firm, they were the softest so far. I liked the YMCA in Taipei. They had doormen who carried your bags, and the front desk people were more pleasant.

Diane was afraid in Taipei, but then she's afraid almost everywhere.

The China tour guide called last night and invited us out for drinks. I declined for us. Diane would have been flustered had she answered the phone.

Love, Pam

HONG KONG - 11 January

Dear Kim:

This trip is going very fast. one city after another. I look forward to Europe because I've allowed myself more time for it. Also. because I'll be rid of Diane.

Her biggest concern in every city is that she didn't like the way she packed her suitcase. and she'll have to repack it again. In my book. if all the stuff fits. close it. and give it to the people at the airport. I throw my stuff in. zip it up. and put it on the luggage cart.

Oh. Hong Kong is a very electric place. I bought you something.

Love ya.

Pam

HONG KONG - 11 January

Throughout my journey I have been very lucky in not having to wait long for transportation.

At Narita Airport, 41 miles from downtown Tokyo, a bus was leaving five minutes after we finished customs. When we arrived in Tokyo, a taxi was at the hotel to take us to the Asia Center of Japan. When we left Tokyo a taxi arrived promptly, so did the airport bus.

In Taipei, I had to wait ten minutes for the airport bus, and was fortunate enough to get the last seat on the bus. When I finally decided to take a taxi to the YMCA, it was there immediately. At the Taipei YMCA I quickly flagged a taxi to the bus station, and the airport bus left three minutes after I got there.

In Hong Kong a taxi was waiting. The ferry came in just as I arrived, going and coming, and the bus to and from Stanley Market was also immediately there. All of this happened without planning. Amazing. Especially amazing was the Stanley Market bus, because there's only one; if you miss it you have to wait for it to come around the other way, which is an hour wait.

Love, Pam

MALAYSIA

Johor
Bahru

SINGAPORE

✪ Singapore

SINGAPORE STRAIT

N
W ✦ E
S

5

I asked for a board
I didn't expect a bed

SINGAPORE - 11 January

Coming into Singapore the plane's view was of the marina and downtown, with pieces of the Singapore River winding through the city. It's clean and beautiful but very humid, 80%. It's the biggest port in the world, measuring tons of goods passing through per year. The water is very clean and blue, you don't see oil all over it.

Water taxis take people from the big ships to the shore, so freighters aren't cluttering the marina.

Love, Pam

SINGAPORE - 11 January

A small outlet of the Singapore River runs behind my hotel, the Riverview. I was expecting it to be a large body of water filled with boats. No boats ever went down the river near my hotel. I did however, have a lovely breakfast outside by the river every morning, once I realized what it was. At first I thought it was a stagnant pool, and that flying bugs would be buzzing around the area. After the first day I realized it was just a very calm, very pretty river outlet, with no mosquitoes.

Love, Pam

SINGAPORE - 12 and 13 January

The Singapore Stopover Holiday from Singapore Airlines includes a Continental breakfast. I was expecting the usual bread and coffee. To my surprise Continental breakfast at the Riverview is an all you can eat buffet. Eggs, bacon, sausage, peanut porridge, pasta, cereal, rolls, croissants, pineapple, watermelon, milk, orange juice, pineapple juice, grapefruit juice, tea, coffee, baked beans, fruit cocktail. After you eat, they make you sign the bill.

There are several restaurants at the Riverview, I thought we had gone to the wrong one and would be billed when we departed. We weren't.

Love, Pam

SINGAPORE - 12 January

Here's a new one for the travel tip books. When Diane and I went to the bank to exchange money today, the teller took Diane's money but refused one of the bills because it was too worn. Diane went ballistic. She couldn't believe they wouldn't take a perfectly good US bill. Neither could I. I'd read where people will reject torn money, but not old money.

Love, Pam

SINGAPORE - 12 January

Orchard Road is the best known street in Singapore, for shopping and business. Most of my time on Orchard Road was spent walking between SwissAir and Singapore Airlines.

After calling the US Embassy, they warned against going to Delhi. Well, actually, all of India. So, I had to change my Delhi flight to a Bombay flight on Swissair. But Singapore Air had put some code on the ticket that I could only get removed in person, so we had to walk to Singapore Airlines to get them to fix the tickets. The lady at SwissAir was afraid she'd have to reissue the ticket, which she did not want to do with a multi-paged Round The World ticket.

Love, Pam

SINGAPORE - 12 January

Dear Mom,

I'm taking a dinner cruise tonight on a Chinese junk boat. Singapore is a beautiful and quiet country. People aren't rushing, and the palm trees remind me of L.A. There are many diverse Malaysian cultures, and here everyone seems to take everything in stride. It's humid, so it seems hotter than it is. We leave for Bombay tomorrow, so I'm drinking all the water and eating all the fresh fruits and veg-etables that I can, while I can.

Love, Pam

SINGAPORE - 12 January

We took a Harbor Dinner Cruise that left from Clifford Pier. We arrived at the pier two hours early, because I thought we could enjoy the water and sit on the pier. It wound up being a place where the local riffraff hang out. The guy from the dinner cruise tour office directed us to a business area that had a large area with grass and places to sit. It was a short walk from the pier.

Love, Pam

SINGAPORE - 12 January

During the Dinner Harbor Cruise on the Chinese junk boat I had a bad headache. Diane gave me some Tylenol it worked for the most part. Mostly, it was hunger, and the rocking of the boat. I couldn't believe that on a two hour cruise they didn't feed us until after an hour had passed.

The food was pretty good, for dinner cruise food. They called it Traditional Singapore food. I liked it all, except the pasta with seafood sauce. The rocky boat bothered me, causing the seafood to be unsettling in my stomach.

Love, Pam

SINGAPORE - 12 January

The Riverview Hotel is very fancy. They turn down our beds at night and leave a chocolate on the pillow. Unfortunately, the beds are too soft for me. By the end of the first night I was sleeping on the floor. The second night I decided to call down for a board for my bed. To my surprise, when housekeeping arrived, I looked out the door and they had wheeled up an entire bed.

I was too embarrassed to have them change the bed. Besides, the guy said the beds were the same, and Diane was already asleep in the bed nearest the door. I

49.

didn't want the noise of changing an entire bed to wake her. So I slept on the floor again.

Love, Pam

JOHOR BAHRU, MALAYSIA - 13 January

The central market is huge and colorful. The tropical fruits are on display, with bananas hanging in bunches suspended on poles in the air. We walked into an area with loose spices in large crates. The aromatic powders that were lingering in the air went up my nose and made me sneeze. I liked this area because the spices were very appealing with their different colors and textures. I could have skipped the butcher area. It was smelly and dirty with blood. The young butcher could tell I didn't like the stench and he laughed at me. I smiled.

Love, Pam

JOHOR BAHRU, MALAYSIA - 13 January

Instead of the Singapore city tour, Diane insisted we take the tour of Johor Bahru, in Malaysia.

The people here are beautiful and of many ethnic mixes. The central market was fascinating. I had a very sweet banana with an extremely thin skin. They say it's the sweetest in the world, and they might be right.

Love, Pam

JOHOR BAHRU, MALAYSIA - 13 January

A typical Malaysian house is built on stilts. The guide said it floods a lot, making stilts a necessity.

The cost of living is low here. Medical cost is 50¢US and the government pays the rest.

The ruling Sultan's house is of Swiss architecture, and the Mosque is colonial, showing the former British ownership influences. We were taken to the Mosque, but everyone was more fascinated with the modern architecture of the Islamic complex next door.

Love, Pam

SINGAPORE - 13 January

Singapore is lovely and peaceful. I took a tour into Malaysia today, someday

I'd like to return there. The people are very warm, and it's very beautiful. I knew Singapore would be the perfect place to stop and take a breath before the hustle and bustle of India.

Diane said Taipei is more crowded than Bombay, I'll find out in about six hours.

Love, Pam

SINGAPORE - 13 January

Today, from 4:30pm to 5:30pm, I rented a taxi to take me to Little India, China Town and the Arab District. Diane didn't go. Diane had wanted to take the Malaysian tour, which we did, and it was terrific. It made me want to come back and spend time in Malaysia. The cultural areas are important to Singapore, and not seeing them would have been missing much of Singapore for me.

The taxi driver wanted $35 Singapore, *$20.60US*, but I bargained him down to $20 Singapore, *$11.80US*, for one hour, and I used the whole hour.

Love, Pam

SINGAPORE - 13 January

One of the last places I saw on my visit was the famous Raffles Hotel. At least I tried to see it. Construction was supposed to be finished six months ago. I had wanted to go and drink a juice and lounge in its restaurant, but restoration proceeds slowly. The taxi driver who drove me by it predicts another year or two. You could see nothing of the hotel except the top part of the roof because they had the scaffolding covered. The roof looks beautiful, and from the photos I've seen it is a grand hotel.

Love, Pam

SINGAPORE - 13 January

I'm sitting in the Business Class lounge in the Singapore Airport about to leave for India. Diane is surprised that I can write postcards so fast. I'm surprised she's so slow. I've written 14 in the last hour. I have the stamps. I don't want to have to purchase stamps in India. That's wasting my money. The lounge is great. It has hot and cold hors d'oeuvres, and a wide variety of drinks. It's the best business class lounge so far.

Love, Pam

SINGAPORE - 13 January

I'm about to leave using Singapore Airlines on my RTW ticket, and use

SwissAir to Bombay. I was delightfully impressed with the service on Singapore Air, the courtesy of thej flight attendants; "Miss Terry may I check your coat," and "what would you like to drink before we take-off," it was fabulous. The meals are endless, and they are delicious. Nevaaz fiancée, Sohrab says SwissAir is the best. I don't know if he's ever flown Singapore Airlines, but they're going to have to move heaven and earth to top these people. If they are at least as good, you will not get any complaints from me.

Love, Pam

BETWEEN SINGAPORE AND BOMBAY ON SWISSAIR - 14 January

I took SwissAir from Singapore to Bombay. I had looked forward to the change because Nevaaz said Sohrab loves SwissAir and flies it whenever possible. I can only think that he's never flown Singapore Airlines. I was underwhelmed with SwissAir, and found their flight attendants and ticket counter people to be very curt, my travel agent says they're just being Swiss. I may take SwissAir back to the states, but I'm not sure yet. It depends on what happens in the Persian Gulf.

Love, Pam

6

Is the bucket for the shower or the toilet?

BOMBAY, INDIA - 14 January

I arrived in Bombay at 1:00am. As usual I picked the slowest immigration line. They would have waived me through customs but I did tell them I had more than $1,000US on me. The form you have to fill out is not only the amount of currency, but the denominations of the currency, and how many of each denomination. I went in the bathroom because most of my money was in my pant's money belt. There was a homeless woman sleeping on the floor, and four of the most disgustingly, filthy, eastern style toilets I have ever seen. The stalls were too putrid to stand in so I stood at the far corner of the sinks. The farthest I could get away from the homeless woman.

I counted and wrote down all the money I had from 12 different countries and all the different denominations. I did not write down the India rupees because it's a restricted currency. I was not supposed to be entering the country with rupees. I was nervous that this homeless woman would come near, but I think she was afraid of me. If I was poor and sleeping on the bathroom floor, I would have come begging.

Love, Pam

BOMBAY, INDIA - 14 January

After I counted my money Diane had to count hers. As we swapped watching the luggage I whispered in her ear, "don't write down the Indian money."

After customs I couldn't find Nevaaz, and I was afraid, because the last thing I was told by a woman on the plane, that loves India, is to watch out for your things because the locals would try to steal anything that you're not holding onto tightly.

Nevaaz was the reason for this trip, we had come to India to attend her wedding.

Nevaaz arrived with a driver and took us to the Sea Green Hotel where there were three homeless men sleeping in the lobby, and another homeless man sleeping outside our door in the hotel hallway. Nevaaz left to go home, leaving Diane and me in the room at the Sea Green Hotel . As I locked the door behind Nevaaz she pointed to the homeless man and said, "he's okay, he's guarding the room." Welcome to India, was all I thought.

Love, Pam

BOMBAY, INDIA - 14 January

After sleeping at the Sea Green Hotel, I tried to call Mom and Dad collect. Later the desk said it wasn't a collect call and that I had to pay for it, 312 rupees, *$16.50US.*

I didn't know how to take a shower in the bathroom. There was a showerhead in the middle of the room and a bucket and a scooper, exactly between the toilet and the shower head. I didn't know if the bucket and scooper were to use after the toilet, since they didn't have toilet paper, or for bathing in the shower. I didn't want to use them for the wrong facility. So, I just washed up in the sink. I was glad I'd packed 3 rolls of Scott 1000 sheet toilet paper.

Nevaaz said the Sea Green Hotel is considered to be one of the nicer hotels in Bombay. I didn't believe it until I read the same thing in my Lonely Planet guide.

We took a walk on the sea side of Marine Ave. A lot of people were either begging, or selling ground peanuts and melons.

Love, Pam

BOMBAY, INDIA - 14 January

Today we moved from the Sea Green Hotel and we were put up in an upper-class apartment belonging to Nevaaz's friend, Behram. He was great, but was recovering from a recent bout with typhoid. I was glad that I'd had the typhoid series of shots before I left home.

Love, Pam

BOMBAY, INDIA - 14 January

Behram's main water line was cut off the first day, so he had collected water in a large trash can. You dip the water into a small bucket and heat it with a heating rod. I didn't realize the rod was akin to tossing an electric curling iron into a bath tub, until the next morning. While sitting on the toilet, I touched my little finger in the water to test for heat and was practically electrocuted. I was stunned. If I had put my entire hand in there, I would have been dead on a toilet in India.

I don't want to die in India.

After that, I took a cold water wash up in the sink. Day two in India without a shower.

Love, Pam

7

Where did all these people come from?

BOMBAY, INDIA - 15 January

We awoke early and boarded a bus the Shroff's, Nevaaz's family, had chartered to go to their family home in the small town of Navsari. It's north of Bombay in the state of Gujarat. The drive will take most of the day.

Love, Pam

BOMBAY, INDIA - 15 January

We were joined by lots of Nevaaz's family and two other non-Indians who had come for the wedding, Carmen and Leila. Carmen is from Iowa and has never traveled abroad. She arrived in India early with Nevaaz's sister, Zarin. They did visit the Taj Mahal, and also the beaches of Gôa. I've seen photos of those beaches, they are gorgeous. I want to go to Gôa someday.

Leila on the other hand is an adventurous 80 year old woman from Hungary but living in Kenya. She was the immigration person who approved the visa so the Shroff's could immigrate to the West.

Love, Pam

BUS BETWEEN BOMBAY GOING TO NAVSARI - 15 January

On the way to Navsari, we stopped at a dairy for tea. This was a mom and pop dairy. I knew nothing was pasteurized here. We had tea. They boil the milk with the tea water in India. I don't like milk in my tea, but we were at a dairy so I thought it would be rude to ask for black tea. The tea was too sweet, but it was also richer than the usual tea with milk. Yesterday I had a discussion about the richness of milk in India vs. the US, with Behram, I told Carmen it was probably buffalo milk. I am not kidding. We stopped drinking the tea.

Love, Pam

NAVSARI, INDIA - 15 January

Navsari is a small Indian town with a large Parsi population. The Shroff's,

Nevaaz's parents, are from here. Nevaaz's mother still keeps a large three story house in Navsari, half a block from her sister's house. Nevaaz's aunt had dinner ready for us when we arrived. She tried to make a portion of the food not too spicy hot. She was so nice but the food was still too hot for me. If you put the meat between bread it cools it down enough.

Love, Pam

NAVSAIR, INDIA - 15 January

At Nevaaz's mom's house several of us had to do laundry. We found three buckets outside and washed the clothes in cold water. Of course, I arrived last and got the rusty bucket with jagged edges. I do not want to get cut or infected in India. I have too much traveling ahead. I washed my shirt very carefully with lavender soap leaves. It was the only thing close to detergent I had brought.

Love, Pam

NAVSAIR, INDIA - 15 January

Once in Navsari we were joined by another American woman, Megan. She traveled to Katmandu, and Delhi/Agra before meeting us here in Navsari. She knew she'd arrive in Bombay after we departed this morning, so she had made reservations to take the train up to Navsari.

They couldn't find her first class reservation at the ticket counter so she had to travel second class. It was crowded and loud because Indian's ride the trains with everything, including the kitchen sink.

Love, Pam

NAVSARI, INDIA - 15 January

We had a black out tonight, right after Nevaaz's family left to go visit another Parsi Temple. We were standing in the dining area when everything went pitch black. Apparently the lights go out for several hours every Tuesday night. Nevaaz's aunt came in with one lit candle and a handful of unli ones. She dripped candle wax on the floor, stood a candle up in the wax and lit the candle. She did this every couple of feet until the room was fairly well lit. The floors in Navsari are cement so this method of lighting the room was practical.

Love, Pam

NAVSARI, INDIA - 16 January

VERY EARLY AM

I never considered the fact that electricity is hydroelectric power, or how the water, hydro, and electric are interconnected, until I came to Navsari. In the middle of the night I had to go to the bathroom. After quite a while I tried to turn the spigot to flush the toilet, but only about a cup of water went into the toilet. Needless to say this wasn't enough. I turned the faucet on the sink, no water to wash my hands. I didn't know what to do. I put the lid down on the toilet and went back to bed.

See Card #2

Love, Pam

NAVSARI, INDIA - 16 January

VERY EARLY AM

CARD #2

Diane went into the bathroom almost immediately after I came out. She was in there for quite a while too. It was going to be whiffy in the morning. The bathroom connected our room with another bedroom. I kept hearing people using it throughout the night. Six adults and two children were sharing this one bathroom.

See Card #3

Love, Pam

NAVSARI, INDIA - 16 January

CARD #3

The water finally came back on at 8:00am. Somebody else flushed the toilet. Apparently because of the black out last night the water in the area doesn't begin to run again until 8:00am. The lights had been on since late last night but it takes awhile for the water to catch up. Hydroelectric power.

Love, Pam

NAVSARI, INDIA - 16 January

Hurray! I finally got a shower in India. A hot wet shower. Once the water came back on I took a long shower. There was no shower curtain, so I left the room very wet.

Love, Pam

NAVSARI, INDIA - 16 January

There were pre-wedding ceremonies which started early this morning, before the rest of us awoke. Some rituals include a priest, which those of us who are not Parsi were not allowed to see. Other ceremonies included an egg, and coconuts, and water, for fertility and happiness.

Nevaaz's family visited a Parsi Temple, which we were not allowed to enter, so Yazdi, Nevaaz's cousin, took us for soda. We didn't notice the people following us until we were inside a store. We got the soda and then saw a mob of people were around us outside the store. There must have been a hundred people. I took out my camera and took pictures. Nobody's going to believe this. From the soda place they followed us like a parade to the bus, and surrounded the bus.

Megan went into the crowds after we were all on the bus. Yazdi suddenly told her to get back in the bus because the crowds were getting too excited.

This also happened later when we went shopping for bangle braclets.

Love, Pam

NAVSARI, INDIA - 16 January

The one great thing about Navsari is that bottled water is cheap. Bisleri water is bottled in Bombay. I was wary of it at first, but so far so good. The local soft drink junk food stand sells Bisleri for 4 rupees, 20¢US, a bottle. Behram paid 35 rupees, *$1.35US* per bottle for us in Bombay. We're stocking up on this stuff to take to Bombay, if the vendor gets a shipment before we leave. We keep cleaning him out everyday.

Love, Pam

NAVSARI, INDIA - 16 January

Meal times are always an adventure for the palate in India. Everyone sits at a picnic table in Nevaaz's aunt's backyard. The 5 non-Indians sit at the far end. Most of us are primarily concerned with developing stomach problems, and have packed an ample supply of immodium.

The usual meal drill for the non-Indians begins as, one person tastes the main dish, while the other four look on intently, waiting for the verdict, like Goldilocks. Too hot, too sweet, pretty good. Too hot and too sweet were the most frequent verdicts.

See Card #2

Love, Pam

NAVSARI, INDIA - 16 January

CARD #2

To the Indians, we are very difficult people to cook for, because we are not accustomed to the strong peppers, and aromatic spices of the region. Even in the United States Mrs. Shroff cooks Indian food everyday, and the Shroff's are accustomed to the very hot spices and peppers. A dish mild enough for us, Nevaaz's aunt would not consider mildly spiced, but downright bland.

Love, Pam

NAVSARI, INDIA - 16 January

Carmen, has the most problems with the food, but she came to India prepared. She packed boxes of macaroni & cheese, and a small jar of peanut butter.

The smallness of the jar of peanut butter was made infinitely apparent this
morning at breakfast. As Carmen thinly spread her peanut butter on a slice of
bread, she commented to me that she had just enough peanut butter to last until
she got to the rest of her food stash in Bombay.
See Card #2

Love, Pam

NAVSARI, INDIA - 16 January
CARD #2

When Carmen sat down at the table Shirin's, Nevaaz's sister's, children, saw
the jar of peanut butter, and decided that's what they wanted for breakfast. That's
when Diane offered them the jar.

Carmen sat there semi-stunned. What could she do? The Shroff's have been
incredibly generous hosts. She watched as her precious peanut butter was
smeared on bread for two sandwiches.

As the jar was about to close, Leila, an older British woman who lives in
Keneya, asked if she could try some. In all her 80 years she had never had peanut

butter. She too was having trouble with the spicy food, and enjoyed the peanut butter immensely.

Surprisingly there was still a little bit of peanut butter left in the jar when it was finally returned to Carmen.

Love, Pam

NAVSARI, INDIA - 16 January

Diane said the bread is good in India, and it is. I really liked the kind of tortilla bread Nevaaz's aunt made. It took away just enough of the spiciness to make pretty tasty mutton tacos.

Love, Pam

NAVSARI, INDIA - 17 January

The Gulf War started today. Nevaaz's brother, Mormazd, told us the news when we woke up. Leila, who's been through every war since WWI, believes this is the start of WWIII. Megan has a transistor radio but can't get any reception, and the TV won't interrupt the soap operas. We get news ten minutes a day from the TV, fortunately it's in English.

Love, Pam

ROAD BETWEEN NAVSARI AND BOMBAY - 17 January

We were on the bus, grateful to be returning to Bombay, only 100 kilometers to go and a bathroom stop to come at the dairy again. Yazdi had just taken down the tea orders when the bus tried to pass a truck that seemed stopped on the road. Suddenly the truck began to make a right turn and another truck was coming. The bus hits the previously stopped truck trying to get back into the lane. The bus spins, goes over an embankment and down into a ditch, tipping halfway over. The steering wheel had come off and the elders who were in the front of the bus went flying into the stairwell and the wall that separates the passengers from the driver. Above it all I heard Nevaaz's blood curdling scream.

See Card #2

Love, Pam

ROAD BETWEEN NAVSARI AND BOMBAY - 17 January

CARD #2

When the elders were thrown, as well as the children, they were piled up on top of each other. I was afraid one very elderly uncle was dead. Fortunately he wasn't.

When people began getting out of the bus, some of them wanted me to get out, but I knew that would be the worst thing I could do for the bus. The people had put the uncle right below me, next to the bus. If I moved and the bus tipped over, it would crush him.

Nevaaz finally composed herself, realized what I was saying and Yazdi and the Mom's brother organized people getting out of the bus in an orderly fashion. One time I ducked my head when I felt the bus move, because I thought it was going to tip over. I prayed, just in case the bus went over. It didn't.
See Card #3

Love, Pam

ROAD BETWEEN NAVSARI AND BOMBAY - 17 January

CARD #3

After everyone was out of the bus, a few of the men got our things out slowly. I, and others had to stand guard to avoid looting. Nevaaz's wedding jewelry, an ornate necklace and matching earrings of 24 karats gold and rubies, were among the packages taken out of the bus.

Carmen took pictures of the bus from all four sides. I wanted too but didn't feel this was the appropriate time to take pictures. I wish I had.

One of the town's men helped us arrange for a flat bed truck. He was very kind, spoke English and reminded me of the comic, Sinbad.

The Shroff's had friends near by, ten minutes by truck. The ride was rough, my foot fell asleep and I put a bad rip in my new pants. I was just glad I didn't rip my skin. I wasn't about to get a shot in a country that Nevaaz admits reuses needles.

See Card #4

Love, Pam

ROAD BETWEEN NAVSARI AND BOMBAY - 17 January

CARD #4

The friends were sweet and just took it in stride when nineteen people unexpectedly showed up at their door. They offered tea. I had iodine drops but I thought it might seem rude or offend our host if I added them for a drink, but I wasn't about to drink water that might be infected with who knows what microrganisms, in the middle of nowhere. This truely was rural India. They had lizards in the house, and I used my first squatter toilet. As you can tell, I'm more than a little paranoid about getting ill over here.

See Card #5

Love, Pam

BUS ACCIDENT NAVSARI TO BOMBAY - 17 January

CARD #5

After the bus accident and getting to the home of the friends of the Shroff's, I used my first steppy, squatter's rights toilet. I had planned to go through my entire trip without using one of these. It was in the house, the floor was tile and there was a porcelain hole in the middle. Don't dare go in such places without shoes on.

Unlike Europe, it didn't have a flusher. There was a bucket and a cup and a spout. After you're done you just swish the floor with a couple of cups of water. See Card #6

Love, Pam

ROAD BETWEEN NAVSARI AND BOMBAY - 17 January

CARD #6

Everything has to be decided by committee with the Parsi's. The accident happened around 4:00pm, the friends lived right by the train station, but they didn't want us to split up. There was a train at 7:00pm that we let pass. The last train was at 9:00pm. At 8:45pm a covered truck came but it was too small for everyone. Six of us were willing to take the train, especially me because of my bad back. But Mormazd and Zarin kept talking by committee. At 8:55pm we left for the train station.

Apparently it's a bad idea to run in small towns in India. So we missed the train by two minutes and had to ride seven hours in the back of a bigger, covered flat bed truck, that somone was able to find.

See Card #7

Love, Pam

ROAD BETWEEN NAVSARI AND BOMBAY - 17 January

CARD #7

Megan had an interesting experience the other day in Katmandu. Every morning they put an English newspaper outside her door. On this day the banner headline said, "Riots in Gujarat." She knew she was going someplace that started with a *G*. She got her note which read Navsari, Gujarat India. She checked every letter of the spelling to make sure. Maybe that's why we're not supposed to run in these small towns.

See Card #8

Love, Pam

ROAD BETWEEN NAVSARI AND BOMBAY - 17 January

CARD #8

I got on the truck last so I could stretch one leg length wise along the gate, but I lived in constant fear that the gate would open. My back pack had only my clothes in it, I'd taken out my Walkman, grateful that I'd brought it.

I laid against my backpack, trying to protect my back. The road was bumpy and the driver drove fast. It was supposed to be a three hour drive, and I had three hours worth of tapes. I figured I'd listen to both tapes and I'd almost be home. Wrong. It turned into a seven hour drive, by the end of which the bumpy road made my back hurt so much, I cried.

See Card #9

Love, Pam

ROAD BETWEEN NAVSARI AND BOMBAY - 17 January

CARD #9

During the truck ride, there were several check points. Since this was a flat bed truck and not a passenger truck, every check point held the possibility that they might make us get out of the truck to find other transportation. At the first check point, Mormazd, bribed them with 15,000 rupees, *$75.00US.*

We were stopped after that, but never had to pay anymore. However, there was a major traffic jam at a diesel stop, as well as, it felt like, a couple of close calls where we almost had another accident, which jangled everybody's nerves.

Also, the odor of fish sometimes permeated the air, and the garbage trucks passed, what a stench. Late night on an India highway.

Love, Pam

8

Wedding cake!
We can eat that!

BOMBAY, INDIA - 18 January

Nevaaz's brother-in-law to be, gave a dinner party for all the out of town guests, and close friends, the night before the wedding. It was in an amazingly beautiful house, and this was just the weekend house. The plants around the pool were exotic, the house looked like an expensive hotel. Nevaaz's sister-in-law to be, is an interior decorator. The dining area had a southwestern flair. The amazing part is that they lived on a part of the beach where you could swim in the water. The tide kept rolling in.

The ocean across the street from Behram's doesn't even seem to move. No one would ever swim in the water by Behram's. I suppose it's telling that it's just down the road from "Cow Patty Beach." At least I thought everyone was saying Cow Patty, actually it's "Chow Patty."

Love, Pam

BOMBAY, INDIA - 18 January

Nevaaz's brother and sister-in-law to be, put out quite a spread for dinner. They had a long buffet laid out on the beach. The food was great, I particularly liked the stuffed crab shell.

The people who attended were fantastic. Friends had flown in from Europe and Africa. There were foreign diplomats, and their spouses, who were assigned to India consulates. Everyone was having great conversation.

Love, Pam

BOMBAY, INDIA - 19 January

I was allowed to go to the wedding. I came all this way and until yesterday I didn't know if I'd be allowed at the wedding. They were going to keep it "family only," but Sohrab kept adding his friends so Nevaaz said her five out of town friends could come.

Love, Pam

BOMBAY, INDIA - 19 January

Sohrab did a beautiful job planning the wedding. It was kept very small, about thirty people. It was held on a large veranda that Sohrab had decorated with a curtain of flowers, strands of orange and white flowers, and green leaves. The centerpiece was a canopy, made of white flowers draped above and behind the area where the bride and groom sat.

The wedding chairs finally arrived yesterday, they are gold leaf with tapestry upholstery. It's a Parsi tradition to decorate the home around the wedding chairs. Behram's parents added a matching couch to their red leather wedding chairs.

Love, Pam

BOMBAY, INDIA - 19 January

When we got to Sohrab's house for the wedding we looked around and spotted a three tier wedding cake. CAKE!!! went through all our brains. Something we could eat. It looked elegant, but more important, delicious, with its white frosting and simple decoration. Our palates had been bombarded by so many different flavors over the past few days, that we could hardly wait for a taste of home.

Love, Pam

BOMBAY, INDIA - 19 January

The wedding ceremony went really fast, about twenty minutes, Nevaaz said it would. It was entirely chanted, of course not in English.

After the ceremony and picture taking it was time to cut the cake. But first there was a champagne toast. We jockeyed for position near the front of the table, close to the cake.

See Card #2

Love, Pam

BOMBAY, INDIA - 19 January

CARD #2

When the cake slices were placed on the table we saw the dark cake. At first we thought chocolate, then we saw raisins and thought carrot. We all chose a large slice and stood in the back of the room to savor and enjoy it. The first fork full went into our mouths and we couldn't believe it. Fruitcake! We were stunned. We just couldn't eat it. I suddenly remembered the British influence in India, and the Brits have fruitcake wedding cakes. We couldn't find a server to give it back so we put the plates on the bookcase and went downstairs.

See Card #3

Love, Pam

81.

BOMBAY, INDIA - 19 January

CARD #3

Downstairs they served a traditional Parsi meal on banana leaves. They had a hot chutney that was good for dipping with a homemade potato chip. They also served sweet noodles with almonds which is a celebratory food, as well as some other dishes I can't describe.

I understand there's just a very subtle difference between Parsi and Indian food. I can't even tell how they are different, but I know I preferred the Parsi food to the Indian.

Love, Pam

BOMBAY, INDIA - 19 January

Nevaaz's wedding reception was on the polo field. 1000 guests were expected, I don't know how many showed up but there were a lot. I wore the mid-length black dress with Kim's long black silk scarf with twenty-four carat gold thread embroidery. It was a hit. One lady asked if the scarf was made in India. I found the tag and it was. I wish I'd known that earlier. I would have asked around for a shop that sells them to get a couple while I was here. They've got to be a lot cheaper here than they are in the states.

Love, Pam

BOMBAY, INDIA - 19 January

Dear Kim,

All the people involved in the wedding want to meet you. Everything I wore was a hit, because of the accessories you gave me. They'd ask me where I got something and I'd tell them, my sister got it for me. I told them, I tell you I need something and you buy it. I just reimburse you for it. Or else, you give me the jewelry as gifts. The black silk scarf was a huge smash, as was my hair with the "wet" hair stuff. You were right, it certainly makes my hair hard. I took pictures. Oh, they really liked the red lipstick. Thanks for everything.

Love, Pam

BOMBAY, INDIA - 19 January

The food at the polo field was incredible. They had booths with different kinds of food: Indian, Parsi, American, Mexican, and more. We headed straight for the American booth. I heard that the reception was catered by the Taj hotel. They did a good job, but they know nothing about how to cook Mexican food. Carmen loved the vanilla ice cream, and was more thrilled when she found out it

83.

was from Kentucky. That meant it was pasteurized!!!

Love, Pam

BOMBAY, INDIA - 19 January

They had a dance floor built on the polo field. I'd heard that Parsi's don't dance but Nevaaz and Sohrab danced the night away. Sohrab's French friends asked all the American girls to dance. I had a good time but I twisted my knee a little, and had to stop, because the dance floor had a downward slope, but we all had fun.

Love, Pam

Ladies in kimonos for New Years, Tokyo, Japan

Devotions hung at Shinto Shrine, Tokyo, Japan

Part of the 1 million people at the Shinto Shrine during New Year's week, Tokyo

Inside a Taoist temple in Taipei, Taiwan.

Soldier standing on pedestal guarding the Martyr's Shrine in Taipei, Taiwan.

Airport bus to downtown Taipei, Taiwan.

View of Hong Kong Island, while going across Hong Kong harbor, in a ferry.

Lady doing exercises by water at Stanley Market.

Kindergarten girls in Shenchen, China, perform dance with fans.

*Shekou, China, Passport Control.
Taking pictures is not allowed in this area.*

Market place in Economic Development Zone, town of, Shenchen, China.

Buddhist monks at monastery in Canton, China.

Singapore Dinner Cruise, food presentation, before serving hungry passengers.

Young woman at entrance to Johor Bahru, she was very kind to me.

Man holding a durian, a Malaysian fruit that smells awful but tastes delicious, Johor Bahru, Malaysia.

Spice crates in the Johor Bahru market place. The fine powers that linger in the air can make you sneeze as you pass by.

Indian women come up to bus window

Sign at Jain Temple, Bombay

Dhobi ghats, where the laundry is done, Bombay, India.

Farm girl, Navsari, India.

Crowds that followed us in Navsari, India.

Man in fur hat is guide at Haydn Church who stopped speaking English, after I showed him my student card asking for a discount, during church tour in Eisenstadt, Austria.

Life size wooden sculptures in Haydn Church.

Pam's perfect purse, from Francis Model's, Venice, Italy.

Bell tower bells in St. Mark's Square, Venice.

Sunrise on the Grand Canal in Venice, Italy.

Overhead view of Venice, from bell tower, Italy.

The Arno from my room with a view, Florence, Italy.

Piano frames at Steinway factory, Hamburg, Germany.

View of Paris from Eiffel Tower, France.

Pergamon altar, Berlin, Germany.

Homeless in 10 year old Old Town in Frankfurt, Germany

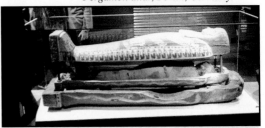

Mummy in Egytpian Museum, Berlin, Germany

9

Let's do breakfast
at the Taj

TOILETS:

Taking a moment out to talk about the toilets in India.

At Behram's, we had to run a hose from the sink spout to the toilet tank and manually fill the toilet tank ourselves after every flush.

With four women using one bathroom this took a considerable amount of time.

In Navsari you had to turn the spout over the toilet then lift the lid to see if it flushed. If it didn't you just turn on the spout a little longer.

The shower in India is the entire bathroom. No stall. The shower head is in the middle of the room, and the entire bathroom gets wet. There's a drain in the floor, somewhere. Bad concept. There's no where at all to put your clothes to keep them dry while you're in the bathroom.

Love, Pam

BOMBAY, INDIA - 20 January

Megan and I went to the tourist bureau to take the city tour, but the rude lady tour guide said it was full.

A cab driver from the Taj Hotel had given Megan a card yesterday, saying that he would give her a tour for 350 rupees, *$15.00US*. So we went to the Taj Hotel, had an all-American food buffet breakfast, and took a wonderful city tour by cab. At one point, while we were at Gandhi's house, we even caught up with the bus tour. The snitty lady tour guide commented that we decided to tour by ourselves. Did she think we were just going to sit around?

The cab driver knew he gave a good tour because he said when we started if we didn't like it we didn't have to pay.

He showed us everything from the hanging gardens, to the dhobi ghats where they wash clothes, India's version of the Chinese laundry, except they wash the clothes by hand, and dry them on the ground on the side of the road. He also showed us the Red Light District. I saw my first Indian transvestite, in a sari.

Love, Pam

BOMBAY, INDIA - 20 January

The taxi driver took us to a Jain temple. I'd seen pictures of gorgeous intricately carved Jain temples in a documentary. This one was much simpler. Unlike the Parsi temples, non-Jains are allowed inside. Before entering there was a large poster, in English, stating the rules of the temple. Rule #1 No woman on her period is allowed to enter. Rule #2 No shoes allowed in temple. I wondered why this sign was in English and not Hindi or some other Indian language.
See Card #2

Love, Pam

BOMBAY, INDIA - 20 January

CARD #2

Having passed rule #1, Megan and I took off our shoes and put them with the other shoes. I recognized that I was in a third world country, and I just laid new Nike's on the pile with sandals, and well worn shoes. I went through the temple quickly, not wanting to temp the locals. My big feet may have been my saving grace.

See Card #3

Love, Pam

BOMBAY, INDIA - 20 January

CARD #3

Inside, the temple was very simple, which was kind of a disappointment after the pictures of huge ornate carved marble and stone I'd seen in pictures. This temple seemed almost austere. People knelt on the floor and said their prayers. It was strange sightseeing while these people were praying. I didn't see any Jain priests. They are instantly recognizable because they walk around completely naked. All and all, I think I'm relieved I didn't see a Jain priest.

See Card #4

Love, Pam

BOMBAY, INDIA - 20 January

CARD #4

It was when we came out of the Jain Temple, that I found out that you have to pay to get your shoes back. The smallest rupee I had was a 100 rupee note, about *$5.00US*, and this wasn't the kind of place that was going to make change. Fortunately Megan had 20 rupees *$1.00US*, which was enough to free both of our shoes.

Love, Pam

BOMBAY, INDIA - 20 January

I mentioned before the taxi driver took us to the Gandhi residence, it is a very interesting, and thorough museum dedicated to his life. They had his spinning wheel on display, that he used to make the homespun cloth he advocated. They also had dioramas featuring his landmark achievements from the beginning of his public life to his murder and funeral.

I learned two words in Gujarat or Hindi, they are "cello," pronounced like the instrument, meaning "let's go," and "pani," meaning "water." I forgot the word for hot, but I was drinking bottled water anyway.

I also learned in India, Marsala is not a wine, but a combination of very hot spices. They use marsala in everything, from food to tea. I didn't even try the marsala dishes.

Love, Pam

BOMBAY, INDIA - 20 January

The food in India comes under two categories for the American palate: too spicy hot, or too sweet. There's a very small bridge between these two, which allow the Americans among us to eat something. The taxi driver who gave us a city tour said, some food is too sweet because the other food is too spicy, and the spices kill the taste buds, so they don't realize that it's too sweet.

Love, Pam

BOMBAY, INDIA - 20 January

I took a taxi to the Catholic church for 5:30pm mass. The taxi driver tried to take me to the wrong church. I didn't know the exact location of the church, but I knew it didn't look like the Catholic church our taxi tour guide had pointed out earlier today, somewhere near the Taj Hotel. I refused to get out of the cab. He asked another taxi driver and took me to the right place. Of course it would have been easier if I'd taken the address with me. But I just assumed the taxi driver would know where the Catholic church was.
See Card #2

Love, Pam

BOMBAY, INDIA - 20 January

CARD #2

I thought it would be a really different experience to hear a Catholic mass in Hindi. I've followed the mass in German, Italian, and Latin in the past. I was stunned when I entered the church and the service was in English. I was also surprised that the service was almost over. The phone book and the nun on the phone said 5:30pm, but they were at the collection and the transubstantiation, with about fifteen minutes of mass left.

See Card #3

Love, Pam

BOMBAY, INDIA - 20 January

CARD #3

I went to communion. After communion they announced that the church bazaar that had been planned for that evening was canceled, in deference to the Gulf War, but you could join them for refreshments in the church hall. I didn't stay for refreshments after church because the sun was setting and I didn't want to be out after dark.

See Card #4

Love, Pam

BOMBAY, INDIA - 20 January

CARD #4

The first cab I flagged wanted to charge me 40 rupees, *$2.00US*, to go to the Air India building. It's a ½ block from Behram's place. I turned him down, grateful I'd remembered to negotiate first. It only cost me 20 rupees, *$1.00US*, to get to the church. The next cab was more difficult to flag down and it was getting dark fast, but he wanted to charge me 200 rupees, *$10.00US*. Maybe he thought I wanted to go to Air India at the airport.

See Card #5

Love, Pam

BOMBAY, INDIA - 20 January

CARD #5

I decided to walk to the Taj hotel and get a taxi, but I got all turned around. The busy night Bombay streets with the traffic and noise were confusing. I finally found a line of taxis but they were all on a break. One finally said he'd take me for 40 rupees. Gratefully, I accepted.

FINAL CARD

Love, Pam

BOMBAY, INDIA - 20 January

Megan is very worried about flying back to the US since the Gulf War has begun. She's booked on a US carrier that takes the European route. She's changing her ticket to anything but a US carrier that takes the Pacific route. A one way ticket is going to cost her a lot of money, but she's hoping her travel agent can fix it when she gets back.

See Card #2.

Love, Pam

BOMBAY, INDIA - 20 January

CARD #2

Megan got a one way ticket on a non US carrier. She's very nervous. She spoke with her boyfriend and he told her to wrap herself up somehow in a sari cloth. Easier said than done. He also said to hide her passport until the absolutely last minute and try not to let anyone see the United States of America on the cover. I'm not nervous, I'm flying the European route, but then again, I'm flying SwissAir.

See Card #3

Love, Pam

BOMBAY, INDIA - 20 January

CARD #3

Megan has Diane really spooked. She flies SwissAir with me to Europe but then she proceeds on to the US via Delta. I've told her she'll be all right. Security is beefed up in Frankfurt with the war and since the Lockerbee bombing. She'll be all right. I hope.

Love, Pam

BOMBAY. INDIA - 20 January

Dear Mom,

India was rough. Between the people leering at me and the bus running off the road. I counted the days until I left. It was good talking to you.

I bought Grandma Davis a silk scarf.

I'm writing this in the airport leaving for Zürich. I did take an exciting city tour today. by taxi.

See ya.

Love. Pam

BOMBAY, INDIA - 20 January

Dear Dad,

I still hurt from the bus accident, and I hurt my knee a little at the wedding dancing. But, I will be all right. I'm glad to be leaving India. I felt so isolated. It would take hours to get a line out to call the US.

Nevaaz's family has been very nice to me. But the people in the rest of the country leer at me, and taxi drivers try to overcharge me, so I walk away.

I'm off to Vienna. I'll see you in six weeks.

Love, Pam

BOMBAY, INDIA - 20 January

Behram ordered mutton cakes and french fries from the country club for dinner, along with bottles of water. Our Navsari water got destroyed in the bus accident. Behram laughs at us for drinking bottled water. The french fries were good and the mutton cakes were, different. They get everything out of an animal while it's alive before they kill it for meat in India. They eat the meat from a lot of old animals in India. Mutton seems to be the most common meat. I'll be glad

95.

to eat a fresh piece of meat soon. One that was bred for that purpose. Consumption.

Love, Pam

BOMBAY, INDIA - 20 January

Carmen, Zarin, Diane and I piled into Behram's little car to go to the airport around 11:00pm. When we got near the airport there was a fork in the road. Everyone said one way but I said the other, and Behram listened to me. A couple of miles down, the road started having a lot of potholes and the airport was no place in sight. Diane got very upset, worried she was going to miss her plane. Behram saw some homeless people on the road and they directed us to the airport. It was down the other fork in the road.

Love, Pam

BOMBAY, INDIA TO ZÜRICH, SWITZERLAND - 21 January

I realized while flying to Zürich that I have the smell of India all over me. I thought it was the guy sitting next to me but I just smelled my shirt and it's me. My clothes reek, Nevaaz warned me there would be smells in India I'd never smelled before. I'm so tired of the smell after a week, I feel like burning the clothes.

When I get to Vienna I'll take a shower and wash my hair. I just washed my hair two days ago, but the dust is unbearable.

I am entering the Western world again.

Love, Pam.

ZÜRICH, SWITZERLAND - 21 January

The plane arrived late from Bombay so I missed my connection to Vienna. That's all right, at least I'm in the Western world again. Diane was able to make her connection for Frankfurt to fly back to the United States.

The staff on SwissAir are not as attentive as the staff on Singapore Airlines. I think I missed the 747's. The meals are not as much of an event either. The plane flight to Zürich was hot, and the man in front of me reclined his chair all the way, for the entire flight.

One good thing, the lady in the business class lounge in the Zürich airport was kind and pleasant to me.

I'm taking Austrian Air from Zürich to Vienna. Even though the delay was SwissAir's fault, I won't get my frequent flyer miles, because they are shifting me to Austrian Air. I don't like that.

Love, Pam

98.

10

Which way do you hold this map?

VIENNA, AUSTRIA - 21 January

I arrived at the Vienna Schwechat Airport and found a van service to take me
to Frau Grün's, at 19 Gongagaza. The driver got me to 1 Gongagaza and asked
me if this was close enough, I said fine. I could certainly walk a few doors down.
I grabbed my luggage cart and walked down a few doors. Suddenly, I was
confused. Every building said 1 Gongagazas, and the street was deserted of
pedestrians.
See Card #2

See Card #2

Love, Pam

VIENNA, AUSTRIA - 21 January

CARD #2

Finally a lady came out of somewhere. I showed her the address and she showed me where on the buildings numbers were, and pointed me four buildings down to, 1 Gongagaza 19. All the buildings had a 1 in front of them because I am in district 1. The building number comes after the street name.

Love, Pam

VIENNA, AUSTRIA - 21 January

Frau Grün met me at the apartment and commented on my lateness. The Austrians are very punctual people. She took me to a room with two beds, but only one had linens on it. The shower is next door to my room, but the toilet is down the hall. It's a treacherous walk over area rugs covering a very slippery hard wood floor, to the toilet.

Except for a man who will depart this evening, I'm the only tenant. With so few tenants, Frau Grün is letting me leave my things here, when I go to Eisenstadt for one day.

Love, Pam

VIENNA, AUSTRIA - 21 January

Frau Grün gave me directions on how to get to St. Stephen's Cathedral and the pedestrian zone on Kärntner Straße, but I made all the wrong turns, starting with my first turn outside the apartment. I finally gave up looking and had a cheap spaghetti dinner, at a small neighborhood restaurant. I asked the waitress for directions to St. Stephen's, and almost immediately got lost, again. I kept walking and it was getting dark. I had no idea where I was. I took a cab back to Frau Grün's. It was less than half a mile, but which way? I was embarrassed by the short trip, but I sure was glad I had a card with her address on it.

Love, Pam

VIENNA, AUSTRIA - 22 January

I'm so glad to be back in civilization. Frau Grün said to walk in Vienna, and I am. It is wonderful, however, I keep getting lost, so I took a city tour today. I took the tour primarily to get my bearings of the city. But I must still be tired from India, because I kept sort of nodding off during the city tour part. It didn't help that the bus was too warm. Second, I wanted the tour of Schönbrunn Palace. I missed that the last time I was here. It was lovely.

Love, Pam

VIENNA, AUSTRIA - 22 January

Schönbrunn Palace, Napoleon's only legitimate son lived and died here of tuberculosis. It is decorated with all the best. Gold leaf, Finnish tapestry, silks, velvets, etc. I didn't see this the last time I was in Vienna because I tried, but failed, to get to Eisenstadt. Schönbrunn is definitely worth the tour.

The tour was in German and English, and our guide was okay. She would tell the German speakers a lot more than the English speakers. I only tipped 10AS, Austrian shillings, that's *$1.00US.*

After the tour, I had an expensive lunch at the Sacher Hotel. It has a reputation for having the best restaurant in Vienna. They are the original creator of the Sachertorte. The Sachertorte has much too much rum in it for me, but it looks like a great chocolate cake with an apricot filling.

Love, Pam

VIENNA, AUSTRIA - 22 January

I wanted the best meal I could possibly have at the Sacher. Meat. Fresh meat was a must. Red meat. The only red meat on the menu today was lamb roll or venison. I didn't really want my meat cluttered with other foods, but I'd been adventurous enough during the past eight days in India, so I wasn't about to try venison for the first time.

The lamb roll was delicious. I even gave the Sachertorte another try. It still has too much rum.

See Card #2

Love, Pam

VIENNA, AUSTRIA - 22 January

CARD #2

Everything was wonderful at the Sacher until I went to leave. I didn't know how much to tip the coat room lady. I tried to keep my voice low and discreetly ask how much is a proper tip. The coat room lady couldn't understand me and started speaking louder, and with the language barrier, our voices carried into the dining room, making it sound like there was a commotion. The maitre d' came out to settle things. It certainly showed my lack of class for the finer things in life.

Love, Pam

VIENNA, AUSTRIA - 22 January

All the trees and gardens are barren in this city that loves its gardens so much. I remember it in the spring, when it is green and the flowers are in bloom. It's beautiful then. Now everything is gray.

Love, Pam

VIENNA, AUSTRIA - 22 January

I had a tour of the Staatsoper, the State Opera house today. The last time I was in Vienna, tours were canceled for the day because of rehearsals. It's a grand building, similar to the Paris Opera House, I don't know if I should be saying that. Very ornate, but tasteful. The way an opera house should be.

Love, Pam

VIENNA, AUSTRIA - 22 January

One hall in the Staatsoper is covered in huge Finnish tapestries that were completed in six years. The curtains are kept drawn and the lights dim so the tapestries don't fade. The hall is used for coffee during intermission, if you have a reservation. Most of the Staatsoper had to be rebuilt after World War II, because of the bombings. It was rebuilt to original specifications, except, the Marble Room.
See Card #2

Love, Pam

VIENNA, AUSTRIA - 22 January

CARD #2

The Marble Room at the Staatsoper, is the only place where smoking is allowed. The pictures on the walls are made from different colored marbles and depict scenes from back stage at the opera. They look like large modern mosaics. I like them. However, I must agree with the critics, that no matter how nice the hall is, the decor doesn't blend in with the rest of the building's design.

Love, Pam

VIENNA, AUSTRIA - 22 January

After my tour of the Staatsoper, I immediately went over to the National Ticket Office to purchase a ticket for my first opera. The tradition in Vienna is to never have the same opera two days in a row, so it changes daily. I was going to go this evening, but the lady at the ticket office was very honest and showed me that I would only see a little of the stage for the 500AS, *$50.00US* maximum, I was willing to spend on a ticket. I decided to buy a ticket for Sunday's opera where I can see the entire stage.

Love, Pam

105.

VIENNA, AUSTRIA - 23 January

I studied my map yesterday, and I was determined to walk to one of the Beethoven houses. I watched the streets carefully so as not to miss a turn. I came across a Haydn apartment, I saw last spring, and realized what I'd done to get lost back then. I finally got to the Beethoven house, I took pictures in the court yard. I noticed people renovating and I thought, don't tell me it's closed. Then I saw the sign, telling me it's on the fourth floor. Of course there's no elevator. And in Europe the fourth floor means the fifth floor. Our first floor is the ground floor. So I climb the five flights of spiral stairs only to find they closed for lunch five minutes earlier.

Love, Pam

VIENNA, AUSTRIA - 23 January

Fortunately at the Beethoven Pasqualati haus apartment the lunch break was only one hour, and not the Viennese 2 ½ hour break.

I sat my butt down on the top step, always ready to write postcards. Suddenly, two Italian workmen, came up and started washing down the stairs so I had to move. I went to the window ledge and they started cleaning the floor around me. I asked if I should move, but I had no where to go, and I wasn't going to go down. He told me to stay and he mopped all the floor around me, then proceeded to the sixth floor. The museum opened up ten minutes late.

The Pasqualati haus apartment is where Beethoven composed the opera "Fidelio," the 4th piano concerto, and a number of symphonies. It has furniture and utensils used by Beethoven, as well as drawings, and music manuscripts.

Love, Pam

VIENNA, AUSTRIA - 23 January

Today I went inside the Haydn-Wohnhaus residence. It was the last place he lived. He wrote "The Creation" in this house. I was the only one there, arriving just after lunch. Much of Vienna closes from 12:00pm to 2:00pm.

I took my time and saw every picture and exhibit. They even have a cast of his death mask. I thought this was a little strange, but it seems to be the tradition.

Love, Pam

VIENNA, AUSTRIA - 23 January

The forte piano of Haydn's is very similar to the one in the Mozart Birth-place house in Salzburg. I do understand what the tourist book says, except for the die hard music lover the houses of the composers will be dull. I love just walking through them, but I know if I'd dragged someone along, they'd be bored stiff.

Love, Pam

VIENNA, AUSTRIA - 23 January

Haydn had the second story built on to this residence. They have drawings of the add-on. The entire second story is open for public viewing. I was disappointed that all the music was photocopied or photographs and not one sheet in his own original hand.

There's a memorial room to Brahms here. Brahms never married because he was in love with Schumann's wife, Clara. I'm not sure why they built a memorial to Brahms in Haydn's residence.

Love, Pam

VIENNA, AUSTRIA - 23 January

I walk the streets of Vienna everyday. My day starts with a walk to St. Stephen's and I go about my day from there. St. Stephen's is in the center of the Ring, the historic section of Vienna. I'm staying near the Donau Canal, at the edge of the Ring. The Donau Canal is an off shoot of the Danube River. The

Austrian name for the Danube is the Donau. It's a ten minute slow stroll to St. Stephen's. Frau Grün said you must walk the streets of Vienna, and she is absolutely right.

Today, I took a new route, looking for crystal necklaces for Kim. It was much quicker. I'd taken it home before but got lost. Now, I can read the map, sort of.

Love, Pam

VIENNA, AUSTRIA - 23 January

Another, "What did I order?" food story.

I wasn't very hungry so I went to the pub next store to Frau Grün's and ordered soup. I had a choice of beef broth with egg or lebarknödelsuppe, liver dumpling soup. I choose beef broth with egg. I expected beef broth with bits of scrambled egg floating around, like hot and sour soup. The broth came, it was pretty good, so I plunged my spoon into the bowl and came up with a raw egg yolk. I didn't know what to do, so I stirred it hoping the hot broth would cook it. Instead it sort of thickened it, but with pepper, it was pretty good.

I did leave the egg membrane in the bottom of the bowl. Next time I think I'll have the liver dumpling soup.

Love, Pam

VIENNA, AUSTRIA - 21 to 24 January

A modern circular, mirrored glass building, the Haas Haus department store and office building, went up across from St. Stephen's a year ago, in Stephensplatz.

I read an article on the plane about the Haas Haus controversy, because it doesn't go with the rest of the historic architecture in the area. They are right. The buildings in Stephensplatz and the surrounding pedestrian zone of Kärntner Straße and Graben are baroque and Gothic in architecture. The mirrored building is an eyesore to the neighborhood. It belongs more in Manhattan than Vienna's Ring. However, it has saved me from getting lost on several occasions because it sticks out into the square. St. Stephen's is obscured until you get into the square because of the angle of the buildings surrounding it. It's hard to believe this because it is a huge cathedral.

Love, Pam

VIENNA, AUSTRIA - 23 January

An older lady in the pub told me how to get to the top of the 19th District. A friend of mine told me about it and it's supposed to be beautiful up there. My knee was bothering me too much to do the uphill climb. Next time. By the way, the woman also wanted me to bring her back a "nice" Hungarian salami if I went to Sapron, Hungary. I'm from L.A. I wouldn't know a "nice" salami from a bad one.

I didn't go to Sapron. The palace I wanted to see was closed for the winter.

Love, Pam

VIENNA, AUSTRIA - 23 January

VIENNA EXPENSE CARD:

Vienna is an expensive city, and my *$45.00US* a day is hard to keep to. Today I figured out I'd eaten only *$10* worth of food. A bus map, transit tickets, city guide book and postage stamps took up the rest of the *$45.00*.

Breakfast was a cup of coffee, the best I've ever had, and a slice of apple strudel for *$5.00*. I had a bratwurst for lunch, *$3.10*, and a snack of some chocolates, *$2.70*. Not having eaten much, I went over my *$45.00*, and ate dinner at the pub next door to Frau Grün's. Fortunately she lives in a area with cheap pub-like restaurants. Fortunately the lady waitress spoke English.
See my next card for another food escapade.

Love, Pam

VIENNA, AUSTRIA - 23 January

Remember last year, when I thought I'd ordered pasta with salmon in Rome, and received lox and toast. This time I thought the sign outside the restaurant translated to steak with oranges. It didn't. Apparently that was some type of mixed drink. The waitress translated and I had Hungarian goulash, with sauerkraut. She insisted on the sauerkraut.

The goulash and sauerkraut were hardy and delicious. According to the menu, it's supposed to be like a soup before dinner, but it was an entire meal. She gave me two pieces of bread, I only ate one. Remembering that in Austria, often, they charge you by each slice of bread you eat. They are not just putting a courtesy basket of bread on the table.

She charged me for the one slice of bread.

Love, Pam

VIENNA, AUSTRIA - 23 January

I've been kind of tired my first few days here. I thought it was just the remnants of the pressures of India, coupled with my knee hurting and getting lost every time I wanted to go back to Frau Grün's. Today I realized, I have jet lag. I

112.

haven't had jet lag the whole trip. I only get jet lag when I go backwards in time. three and a half hours difference from India, is like New York to L.A. I thought I was just lazy.

Love, Pam

11

... then he stopped speaking English

EISENSTADT, AUSTRIA - 25 January

While taking the Austrian equivalent of a Greyhound bus from Vienna to Eisenstadt, I kept trying to figure out the names of the towns where the bus was stopping, and where the signs were posted. The bus kept stopping at places that looked like normal bus stops.

Suddenly, I saw a sign, Eisenstadt, 3 kilometers, but when the bus stopped it was in the middle of nowhere. There was no phone or taxi, so I didn't get off. I didn't even know where the bus route ended. Unlike the bus at the bus station when I bought my ticket yesterday, this bus didn't have a sign saying Eisenstadt. I thought after all this time, I'm going to miss the town again.

Love, Pam

EISENSTADT, AUSTRIA - 25 January

I finally made it to Eisenstadt. It took nine months, since my original attempt, but I made it. I came into town on a bus which stopped in every podunk town, of which Eisenstadt is one. There were several stops in Eisenstadt and I didn't know where to get off. A woman on the bus asked me if I spoke English. I couldn't believe it. I thought I wreaked American.
See Card #2

Love, Pam

EISENSTADT, AUSTRIA - 25 January

CARD #2

The woman on the bus could tell I was lost. She told me we were in Eisenstadt and to get off at the end of the line. Then she proceeded to point out all the Haydn places of interest. She was obviously proud of her town, because I hadn't told her what a Haydn lover I am.

She laid out the town for me, the Old Town Monument, the hotels and restaurants, then the working class section.

Love, Pam

EISENSTADT, AUSTRIA - 25 January

After the lady directed me where to get off the bus, I didn't know where to go to find my hotel. I had made reservations through an Austrian, Burgenland travel bureau, long distance. I had an address, RusterStraße 51, but no directions on how to get to the hotel.

There wasn't a taxi anywhere. I didn't even know if they had taxis in this small town. I stopped a local lady who happened to speak English. It must have been difficult to explain where the hotel was because she decided she was going that way and she would drop me off at the hotel. This was great, except I still don't know how to get back to the bus depot tomorrow.

Love, Pam

EISENSTADT, AUSTRIA - 25 January

The hotel I'm staying at is the Gasthof Café Ohr. It's the perfect atmosphere for a small town. It's a simple place with rooms above a restaurant, but for *$1.00US* more than Frau Grün's, I have my own bathroom and CNN. It's the first news I've had of home since the Gulf War started. Also, there's wall to wall carpeting, and non-skid tile in the bathroom.

The woman behind the desk is very nice, and has a better command of English than she thinks. She has been very helpful. I think I may be the only tenant here, also, I'm not sure yet, bit it's not full.

Love, Pam

EISENSTADT, AUSTRIA - 25 January

After settling into The Gasthof Café Ohr, the woman at the desk directed me to all the places I wanted to go. She told me to walk along the one road that runs in front of the hotel, and they will all be on it. That was easy, I could guarantee at least for one day in Austria, I wouldn't get lost.

She was correct, the spots were all along RusterStraße. But in true Austrian style, the road did change its name to EsterházyStraße half way up.

Love, Pam

EISENSTADT, AUSTRIA - 25 January

My first stop on my Haydn self tour was the Esterházy Palace. It's where Haydn was court director for 31 years plus.

When I got to the Esterházy palace I followed the information sign to a

117.

multi-language information telephone. It gave some facts about the palace, but not enough, and it cut you off before the end.

After listening to the multi-language information phone, I looked forward to a tour. Especially to see the Haydn room, where concerts are held in the summer. It's said to have the second best acoustics in Austria, and beautiful Italian frescos on the walls and ceiling. The Musikverein's Goldensaal in Vienna has the best acoustics in Austria.

Love, Pam

EISENSTADT, AUSTRIA - 25 January

I went inside the palace office and asked for a tour. The lady promptly turned me down. I had read in a guide book, if you have four people for a tour in the winter you could have a tour. I was prepared to pay four fares just to see it. Wrong. Instead it's ten plus people and it has to be planned ahead so they can arrange for a guide.

After being told I couldn't have a tour, I pulled my, "I came all the way from America just to see this. Can't I, at least, see the Haydn room?" I saw a flash of weakness in the lady's eyes, so I added "Two minutes."

She took me up.

Love, Pam

EISENSTADT, AUSTRIA - 25 January

It was cold inside the Esterházy Palace, but I didn't care. I was too excited at the opportunity of seeing the Haydn room. I had never even heard of the Haydn room before the information phone described a grand room.

The woman opened the doors. At first I was a little disappointed after the phone description. As she opened another set of doors I realized this was just a foyer. I walked through the other doors into a grand hall. It's the first time I'd ever seen framed frescos on a ceiling before. The wood floor is the original, installed during Haydn's lifetime.

It only seats 500 people, but prices are *$40.00US* tops, unless as sometimes happens, someone like Jose Carreras sings in the hall. Then tickets were equal too, *$100.00US*. They could sell the hall three times over. It's a wonderful hall. I want to see a concert here.

I took photos inside and the lady took a picture of me.

Love, Pam

EISENSTADT, AUSTRIA - 25 January

Except for two pictures at Frau Grün's, I hadn't used my tripod and self-timer until today in Eisenstadt.

I took pictures of myself in front of the Esterházy Palace and in the court yard. I hope they come out. People passing looked at me a little funny, then let me go about my business.

Later I took a picture in front of the Haydn Church. It may look funny, but I think it's kind of ingenious when traveling alone, to take along a tripod, and camera with a self-timer, so you can take pictures of yourself at places you visit.

Love, Pam

EISENSTADT, AUSTRIA - 25 January

After the Esterházy Palace, I went to the Landesemuseum. A Haydn Museum is there. Also the lady from the bus told me there was a Haydn organ inside the main museum. Of course, I got there at 12:05pm and the museum closed for lunch from 12:00pm to 1:00pm. So a local café lucked out and got my business. It was really just a bar with tables. All the waitress could offer were wurste, sausages, or ham and eggs. I took the ham and eggs; they were good, except the eggs were sunny side up, and a bit undercooked. I ate them anyway. They serve them with pickles. They seem to like pickles a lot, both in Austria and Germany.

Love, Pam

EISENSTADT, AUSTRIA - 25 January

I got to the Landesemuseum at 1:07pm. The door was still locked for lunch, but there was a door bell, so I rang it. I didn't even ask to see the Haydn Museum it houses, I knew when I went to Eisenstadt that it was closed for the winter. Besides, the guy didn't speak English, and didn't want to be bothered.

I did see the Haydn organ. It was powder blue and very tall. Of course I couldn't touch it to hear how it sounds. There was also a terrific exhibit of Franz Liszt's room, complete with a piano near to looking like today's modern piano. I forget how relatively new the modern piano is among musical instruments.

Love, Pam

EISENSTADT, AUSTRIA - 25 January

Literature I got from the Esterházy Palace gave me a scare, I knew I couldn't see the Haydn museum, but this paper said I needed an appointment for the Haydn Church, Bergkirche. I found a phone in the Landesemuseum and the man at the church said come right over.

The man was in the church when I arrived. He spoke broken English but I understood him.

Love, Pam

EISENSTADT, AUSTRIA - 25 January

The Bergkirch, Haydn Church, is the main reason I wanted to come to Eisenstadt, I'd seen this church in a Czernig etching I've owned for five years. It is part of a series of etchings I have of places where famous German and Austrian classical composers, like Mozart, Haydn, Schubert, and Beethoven liked to compose their music. I want to see as many of these real places as possible. Some of them were destroyed in WWII.

See Card #2

Love, Pam

EISENSTADT, AUSTRIA - 25 January

CARD #2

Surprisingly, the fence in front of the Esterházy Palace may be in another etching. Haydn loved Eisenstadt, it is a lovely little town. He wanted to live and die here. Although he spent his last thirty years here, he died in Vienna.

His body was returned shortly after his death but his head was soon stolen. It took 154 years for his head to be returned from Vienna to Eisenstadt. The Viennese had his head on display in a museum, where people could go and touch the top of his head. Yuck.

Love, Pam

EISENSTADT, AUSTRIA - 25 January

You enter the interior of the church from the back. From the front you enter a very small chapel that was added later, I think. Not much later, because it matches beautifully. The difference is that, the frescos in the chapel were done by Austrians.

The church has another organ that Haydn played regularly. It was also used by Beethoven and Schubert. Such history. It's a beautiful, comforting, church. Small. There was a rope between the first rows of seats so you couldn't approach the altar, but I'm fairly sure they have masses here.

Love, Pam

EISENSTADT, AUSTRIA - 25 January

After leaving me alone in the Haydn church for five minutes, the man came back and let me into the Haydn mausoleum. It is creamy white, made of cararra marble. He explained that the statues surrounding it were each of the four seasons in honor of Haydn's oratorio "The Seasons."

He hummed the tune carved on the palcard of one of the angels on the casket, if that's the proper word for it. A light shined through the ceiling dome and the seven last words of Christ surrounded the hole where the light shined through, in tribute to Haydn's "Creation" and "Seven Last Words" oratorios.

I took pictures. It may be morbid, but I also had my picture taken next to the casket.

Love, Pam

EISENSTADT, AUSTRIA - 25 January

As I was finishing at the mausoleum, six Germans, or Austrians, joined us and the man decided to collect a 15 shilling fee. I showed him my student card and he motioned I didn't have to pay. However, the man also stopped speaking English after that.

In actuality, I had already put money in the collection box when the man had left me alone in the church. I didn't have any more small bills, and I knew he couldn't make change, so I just followed the group.

See Card #2

Love, Pam

EISENSTADT, AUSTRIA - 25 January

CADR #2

After Haydn's mausoleum, the man asked if I wanted to see the Kalvarienberg, Calvary section. The Germans knew what he was talking about. I didn't, but I was game for anything. The Calvary part of the church is in caves, or catacombs, under and around the church. It is a monument to remember what happened to Jesus Christ on the route to Calvary to be crucified. In the Catholic church they are known as the 14 stations of the cross. The Kalvarienberg depicts 24 stations, from the bottom of the church to the steeple.

They are amazing, life-size painted wooden sculptures, of Jesus, St. Veronica, Mary, and others in the caves. It is dark, and they are lit between the rocks in front of the caves.

Love, Pam

EISENSTADT, AUSTRIA - 25 January

The Calgary section leads to the outside tower of the church. At one point the man looked at me thinking I wouldn't want to walk the 160 steps to the top. Insulted, I looked at him and said, "I'm going up." I got to the top when everybody else did.

Fortunately, it was a beautiful day, sunny and clear. The first such day I had had in Austria. You could see forever. I took one picture of the town and had someone take a picture of me.

My knee hurt on the way down, and a lot on the way home. But I did it.

Love, Pam

EISENSTADT, AUSTRIA - 25 January

There are taxis in Eisenstadt. I had the woman at the front desk call one to pick me up. I didn't wait for her to tell the driver to take me to the bus station. I instead met him outside and told him myself I wanted to go to the busbahnhof, certain that was the German word for bus station.

He drove off and took me to some deserted shack with empty buses. I knew this wasn't the place, so I didn't get out.

See Card #2

Love, Pam

EISENSTADT, AUSTRIA - 25 January

CARD #2

I tried to explain I wanted the bus for Vienna, Wein, in German. He thought I wanted him to drive me the 31 miles to Vienna. This hardly fit into my *$5.00US* bus budget, for returning to Vienna.

Suddenly, I saw a lady and beckoned her to come over to the taxi. She didn't really speak English, but she seemed to understand where I wanted to go. She told the taxi driver something in German, and he drove off.

This time he dropped me off at the correct bus station.

Love, Pam

VIENNA, AUSTRIA (IMMEDIATELY AFTER EISENSTADT) - 25 January

I can't believe it. In Eisenstadt the lady at the hotel said postcards cost 7 shillings to mail to the USA. I thought she was wrong but I couldn't remember if the postcards I'd mailed from Vienna took 7 shillings or 7.50 shillings. Before I mailed the postcards from Eisenstadt I double checked the postage at a tobacco shop. That's where you buy stamps in Europe. He also said 7 shillings. So I mailed 17 postcards from Eisenstadt.
See Card #2.

Love, Pam

VIENNA, AUSTRIA - 25 January

CARD #2

I just arrived back in Vienna and went to the post office in the bus station, just to check the USA postcard price one more time. The postal woman said it cost 7.50 shillings. 50 groschen more, *5¢* per card more. Because of the Eisenstadt mistake she says my postcards will end up in the dead letter pile. All my memories. All that time trying to get to Eisenstadt. I can barely write this I'm crying so hard.

Love, Pam

12

"To go" is a dirty word

Never to lose out on a money making opportunity, Vienna's transit service has prices for people who ride with their dogs. The dogs pay children's rate. Vienna must rival Paris on people with dogs, but in Vienna, they are not just petite dogs, but are up to German Shepherd size. What they need in Vienna is a "Poop Scoop" law. Or like in Paris, someone whose job it is to pick it up.

I learned a new term today, "Academic time." If you're invited for dinner, you should never show up on time. Show up fifteen to twenty minutes late, to give the cook extra time. Thirty minutes is pushing it, an hour is rude.

Love, Pam

VIENNA, AUSTRIA - 26 January

Last night I went to my first opera, *Pelléas & Méllisand.* I wasn't expecting to be enthralled by it because it was Debussy.

I don't care for his symphonic music. It was nice, but it was ethereal, with airy music, and the effect of misty water floating on the stage. One man later told me, "if you can sit through *Pelléas & Méllisand* as a first opera, and not walk out, you can sit through any opera." I'd like to see another opera. A robust Italian one next time.

The excitement came before the opera. They print the tickets in military time, and I had counted half a dozen times and come up with 8:00pm. At 6:15pm I was about to take a nap when I saw the ticket and counted one last time. The opera started at 7:00pm.

I put on my dress, couldn't find my jewelry. Ran out the door and made it with five minutes to spare, even though the tram ran slow. I did wind up wearing my tennis shoes.

Love, Pam

VIENNA, AUSTRIA - 27 January

I almost started an international incident today. Twice.

First, I needed to take some aspirin, so on my way to the Burgkapelle, that's the palace chapel at the Hofburg Palace, I stopped at the Dom Café coffee house, in Stephensplatz. I asked for a melange, coffee with steamed milk, like a café au lait. Then I said those two American words, "to go." Every waitress and staff person in the place got up in arms. I finally decided to sit down and drink it quickly.

See Card #2

Love, Pam

VIENNA, AUSTRIA - 27 January

CARD #2

The second incident occured at the Burgkapelle. I was one of the earliest people in line at the Burgkapelle, for the Vienna Boy's Choir. Unfortunately, it turned out I was standing in the wrong place. Nothing is marked, so the tourist won't know where to go. When the right line was established I wound up near the end of the line. I had been waiting an hour when the line switched. I didn't see anything wrong when I asked a man near the head of the new line to buy me a cheap seat. He was very put off by this request.

See Card #3

Love, Pam

VIENNA, AUSTRIA - 28 January

CARD #3

I went to see the Vienna Boys Choir mass today. The man who was put-off by my request to buy me a cheap ticket bought me a ticket as a gift, giving it to me very discretely. The lady behind him was mad even though she didn't say anything. I was there first, just standing in the wrong place, but people don't ask others to buy seats in Vienna.

The cheap seat was so bad that all I could see was a wall, with bordello red satin wall paper. No alter. I went down to standing room. Only thirty people are suppose to be allowed to stand. I stopped counting after one hundred. The people in standing room don't stand along the side walls, they stand down the middle of the center aisle. It was a spectacle. I left. Next time I'll buy a good ticket.

Love, Pam

VIENNA, AUSTRIA - 27 January

You can tell all the tourists are out today because we all walk around holding maps trying to figure them out. I was up early trying to see the Vienna Boys Choir, and tourists were already out. Walking with maps, on the tram with maps, and of course, I had my very well worn map with me, and looking at it.

The mass of the Boy's Choir was disappointing. I tried to find the English speaking church on my map. No luck. Also, it started snowing.

Love, Pam

VIENNA, AUSTRIA - 21to 27 January

The *You Should Be Ashamed To Wear Fur* people obviously haven't found their way to Austria, or else the ammunition on display in hunting stores in Eisenstadt is there for a reason. All the woman have fur coats, and men and woman all have fur hats for the winter. Some of it may be fake, but I don't think much of it is.

Love, Pam

VIENNA, AUSTRIA - 27 January

I finally got to the Fine Arts museum that was recommended to me. There was a lot there and I had to go to the bathroom so I think I missed a few paint-ings.

The *Group of Theseus* sculpture by Antonio Canova was a striking entrance piece for the museum. It's made of white marble, and depicts a warrior wielding a club above his head, ready to attack the collapsed half man half horse he has held down by the neck with his knee lodged in the man's kidneys. It sits at the top of a grand staircase as you enter the main body of the museum. A wonderful place to display it.

There's still so much I have to see in Vienna. What a wonderful reason to return. Anybody want to come along?

Love, Pam

VIENNA, AUSTRIA - 27 January

The Habsburgs put this museum collection together while they ruled Vienna. It's a grand building with frescos on the ceiling, Egyptian and Etruscan artifacts, sculptures, and paintings.

I only had a short period of time, so I decided to see the paintings and save the rest for another visit. Wonderful painted masterworks of Vermeer, Titan, Valázquez, Rembrandt, and Rubens are displayed on the third floor. I particularly liked the painting *Children's Games* by Pieter Breughel the Elder, where the children take over the town.

It seems to be a custom in the large museums in Vienna to have a coffee café. I had a melange and strudel. The strudel wasn't so great. The café was laid out very open in the middle of the museum.

By the way, that *International Student Identity Card* has come in very handy on museum and tour discounts.

Love, Pam

VIENNA, AUSTRIA - 28 January

Today was my last day in Vienna. Wouldn't you know it, it was one of those days when everything went wrong. I woke up only wanting to wash my clothes. A laundromat seems to be foreign to the Viennese. I was told by the tourist bureau that none exist in the Ring, but there's a self-service laundry in the Ninth District. I went up there and the lady said, it's 226 shillings for two loads. That's *$22.00US*, I kid you not. Then the lady pronounced "That includes soap too."

Needless to say, I took my dirty clothes with me to Italy.

By the way, I told this price to a regular citizen and she said it was correct.

Love, Pam

VIENNA, AUSTRIA - 28 January

I'm tired of carrying all this luggage, I'm sending half of it home. I got a box from McDonald's, put half my stuff in it plus one of the canvas suitcases. I reinforced the bottom of my other canvas suitcase with the hard bottom piece

from the one I packed. I'm sure glad it was removable. I would never have found
a box big enough to fit a suitcase, and at this point I'd have of thrown it away.
See Card #2

Love, Pam

VIENNA, AUSTRIA - 28 January

CARD #2

I put the box on my luggage cart and went to the main post office. Fortunately the postal clerk spoke English, but he refused to take my box. He said I
needed tape, and they didn't sell any. He told me I'd have to go to the paper store.
I traipsed through the streets with this box on a cart trailing behind me and I
found the paper store.

On the way back to the post office, a big truck drove fast, through a big
muddy puddle, and splashed my heavy coat.
See Card #3

Love, Pam

VIENNA, AUSTRIA - 28 January

CARD #3

Once back at the post office the English speaking guy had left. No one else
spoke any English. The forms were in French and German, and there were lots of

forms. I tried to translate them using my limited French, but there were more words I didn't know than I did. I tried to send it slow boat so it arrives home when I do. After all those forms I'm not sure I'll ever see my stuff again.

Love, Pam

VIENNA, AUSTRIA - 28 January

In keeping with things going wrong today, I had planned my day around the 3:00pm tour of St. Stephen's Cathedral. Three days ago, I saw a French tour outside and I was told the 3:00pm is in English. When 3:00pm came, this guy came out and said it was in German. I thought it would be in German and English like my city tour, but he adamatly said it was only in German. For emphasis he added that all the tours were only in German. Of course he said all this in perfect English.

There was no arguing with this guy. However, they are doing some major restoration to this church and they have collection boxes all over the place. It would behove them to give tours in several languages.

Love, Pam

VIENNA, AUSTRIA - 28 January

Dear Mom,

I hope you'll want to come to Vienna with me one day. I think you'll love it the way you loved Florence. What Florence is to art, Vienna is to classical music.

I'm writing this in the train station waiting to go to Venice. I hope I do this right. I don't want to end up in the wrong car and get disconnected from the train. You know of course, I was too cheap to buy a sleeper car, or a couchette.

Love, Pam

13

I hope this pigeon doesn't poop on my coat

VENICE, ITALY - 30 January

I didn't miss my stop in Venice but I almost got off at the wrong stop. The train was slowing down to pull into the Venice train station, I grabbed my things and anxiously dashed for the door. I verified with the people at the door "Venice, Venezia." I was ready to get off that train and see those canals, but the Italians by the door told me "No, not here." I did not understand and started to get off. "No not here, the next stop," they said again. I didn't understand. The sign said Venezia-Mestre, that meant Venice. I don't know why but I listened to them and stayed on the train. As the train pulled off I didn't see any canals just industrial smoke stacks and factories.

A few minutes later the train pulled into Venice-Santa Lucia. I walked to the end of the platform and saw the waters of the Grand Canal at my feet. If you weren't looking you could walk straight ahead and fall right into the water.

Love, Pam

VENICE, ITALY - 29 January

My main reason for going to Venice, aside from the fact that it's a beautiful city, was to have a tour of St. Mark's Basilica. When I came with a tour before, I was very upset that we got a tour of the glass factory but not the Basilica.

This time the full moon was against me. I arrived at 8:30am by the time I figured everything out, and got the vaporetto, a boat that is the Venice equivalent of a bus, I got to my hotel at 10:00am. In the off season, they only have one tour, at 9:30am.

Love, Pam

VENICE, ITALY - 29 January

Never ever think Pam is down for the count. When I couldn't get a tour of the Basilica, a lady at the American Express office, refered me to a book store. The man there sold me a book on Venice, with a chapter on the Basilica complete with diagrams and explanations. I used it, and it was better than any tour could have been. A French guy there was doing the same thing, but his book wasn't as good. So I helped him a little.

Love, Pam

VENICE, ITALY - 29 January

I found my way to the leather shop, Francis Model. I love this place. It's primarily a purse and belt shop. Beautiful, unique, yet classic purses. It's a mom and pop shop, he makes them, she sells them. She speaks English, he doesn't. She wasn't there today, but the signor and I managed to communicate. He showed me half a dozen purses, most too big for my taste. Then he showed me a perfect Pam purse.
See Card #2.

Love, Pam

VENICE, ITALY - 29 January

CARD #2

The purse at Francis Model was medium dark brown leather, with a long thin shoulder strap, and a big antique looking brass clasp on top. I really wanted it.

141.

I've never seen anyone with a purse like this. Unfortunately, the body of the purse was bulky, shaped kind of like a football, and I would have to squash it in my luggage. I didn't buy it.

See Card #3.

Love, Pam

VENICE, ITALY - 29 January

CARD #3

I did however have an ingenious idea, or at least I thought it was ingenious. I took a picture of the purse, thinking I'd send him the picture and enough money to cover the cost of the purse plus postage. After I took the photo, the signor did his best to tell me that they've had trouble mailing things in the past so they don't ship. Oh well.

Love, Pam

My friend Tomiko went to Venice in the spring, I gave her the picture, money, and the best directions I could. She found Francis Model but didn't see the purse. When she showed the signor the photo he remembered me and the purse. Fortunately he had moved it to the back room. It's still one of my favorite purses.

VENICE, ITALY - 29 January

I decided to be very touristy and have my picture taken in front of the church. Of course I only had my picture taken because I was able to bargain the price down. There were pigeons flying all around, and on me. One pigeon landed on my sleeve. My only thought was I hope this bird doesn't poop on my coat. It's too cold to part with it for a day to have it cleaned.

I read in the Frommer's book that one of the things to do in Venice was to go to the top of the Bell Tower in St. Mark's Square. So I went to the top of the tower. *$3.00US*. The city view was spectacular, you could see the labyrinth walkways below. The view of the water was very brown and hazy. I took out my tripod and took pictures of me from there.

Love, Pam

VENICE, ITALY - 30 January

Venice at night, in the winter, and in the early morning when the sun is down, gets very deserted, except for a few locals here and there. The hardest part was finding a place open for dinner. I finally got a lousy cheeseburger at a pub in St. Mark's square.

My Venice accommodations were not good for me. Alloggi Ai Do Mori is up endless flights of very steep stairs. There must have been five flights of stairs. Good thing I left my luggage at the train station and put a change of clothes in my daypack. The pensione had cots for beds that would wreck the best of backs, a cheap folding chair and a heater that didn't work. I froze as I slept on the floor.

I remembered an old back packing trick and slept with my hat on trying to keep warm.

Love, Pam

VENICE, ITALY - 29 January

It was freezing cold at the Alloggi Ai Do Mori. I turned the radiator knob all the way to the right and waited an hour. No heat. I turned it all the way to the left and waited an hour. No heat. I put it half way. No heat. I looked for something else that moved. Nothing. I was shaking so much trying to keep warm that I had to keep getting up to go to the bathroom.

Love, Pam

VENICE, ITALY - 30 January

I woke up very early, finally giving up on getting a good night sleep. I took a shower, Alloggi Ai Do Mori has showers like India, where the whole bathroom is the shower. The owner thinks it's more efficient.

I sneaked out of the pensione while it was still dark outside. I had paid them by mail before arriving. I went to the vaporetto dock but the ticket booth was closed.

The vaporetto came in ten minutes, I boarded the boat and sat down inside trying to blend in but there were only a handful of people on the boat. I waited for someone to ask for a ticket. I'd heard there is a hefty fine if you are caught riding without a ticket. Nobody ever asked for a ticket.

When the vaporetto pulled up to the train station dock I rushed off. Lucky break.

Love, Pam

14

Wait! My clothes are in there.

FLORENCE, ITALY - 30 January

The train pulled into Santa Maria Novella, Florence's train station, at noon. I got off the train, immediately got a city map and headed for the laundry. I walked through the streets of Florence with my luggage on a luggage cart. I arrive at the laundry and when he said it would be ready by 6:00pm, I put every piece of clothing I had in his basket. It cost me *$23.00US*. Okay, so Vienna wasn't more expensive, but at least here they did the laundry for me. In Vienna I'd have to do the laundry myself for *$22.00*.

That evening I took the local bus sightseeing and got lost. I read the bus map wrong. I got to the laundry just as he was locking the door. He did give me my laundry. Whew.

Love, Pam

FLORENCE, ITALY - 30 January

I arrived in Florence, dropped off my laundry and got bus #23 just as Frommer's said I should. I read the bus map, it said there was a stop at Ponte alla Grazie. I thought the bus signs at the bus stop were saying the name of the stop on top. I was wrong. I missed my stop by a long shot. I spent an hour on the bus going from one end of the line to the other before I finally got off at the right stop.

Even after I'd asked the conductor he didn't call out the stop, and I almost missed it again.

Love, Pam

FLORENCE, ITALY - 30 January

Finally getting to my hotel, Pensione Rigatti, I found I did get the room with a view that I requested. I can see the Arno, Ponte Vecchio, and Piazzale

Michelangelo. There are rowers on the Arno almost always during daylight hours. At 6:00pm the church bells go off every night.

My room is on the third floor, and there's even an elevator. The bed is soft, but sleepable, and there is a midnight curfew.

Love, Pam

FLORENCE, ITALY - 30 January

Since I am going to be in Florence for several days I decided to ask if it's possible to get a board for my bed. I wasn't really expecting anything but asking couldn't hurt. This is a larger pensione than the other places I've stayed, about 30 rooms, so I thought she might have a board somewhere.

The house boy just arrived with a solid wood board that must be an inch thick. I haven't had a bed this hard since India. I'll sleep well tonight.

Love, Pam

FLORENCE, ITALY - 31 January

It is nearly impossible to cash a US travelers cheque in Florence. The dollar is doing so bad that by the time the bank can turn it in they've lost money. I was shocked when banks turned me down and sent me to competitor's banks. It took me three banks before someone would change my travelers cheques into lira. I'll have to go to American Express next time.

Love, Pam

FLORENCE, ITALY - 31 January

It took nine extra months but I finally saw the real *David*. None of the copies in the area compare to it. I looked at it for a long time, and I walked around it. Sculpture should always be seen from all sides. There was a poster telling of the lighting challenges of such a great piece of art. The Galleria dell' Accademia, Accademia Gallery, presents it wonderfully well.

When I came to Florence with a group tour they showed us every copy of *David*, but we arrived too late to see the real one. I felt cheated then, and today I know for certain I was cheated.

Love, Pam

FLORENCE, ITALY - 31 January

Right before the *David* there are about six unfinished sculptures by Michelangelo. The *Palestrina Pietá* is one of them. It was really quite marvelous,

149.

you can feel the weight of Jesus' body on Mary's and the Apostle's.

Correction: The Palestrina Pietá is not by Michelangelo, and the "Apostle" is Mary Magdalen. I guess my lack of knowledge is showing. However it is by an unknown student of Michelangelo's, and even the experts were fooled for centuries.

There is always something new and wonderful to see in Florence museums. Before the unfinished sculptures there was the last work of Giambologna, *The Rape of the Sabine Women.* It's a beautiful, though violent, complicated sculpture, the way the bodies of the women and men contort among each other. Again, it must be seen from all sides to truly be appreciated.

Love, Pam

FLORENCE, ITALY - 31 January

After the *David*, the Accademia Gallery has this room full of marble statues. It's almost like a warehouse there are so many. I noticed that most of them had black dots, like freckles on them. A guard, in limited English, was able to tell me that these were models, and the dots were sizing marks in order to make a bigger, completed statue, exactly like the model.

Love, Pam

FLORENCE, ITALY - 31 January

Dear Kim,

I was glad to here you received the birthday card I sent you.

I went to the Duomo Museum today. After reading on the back of a postcard that it has a Michelangelo *Pietá* where he made himself Nicodemos. It sits alone at the top of the first flight of stairs. It is a beautiful unfinished *Pietá*. Michelangelo's last. Mary was worked on by a pupil, you can tell. There was no left knee on Jesus, just a hole, maybe the years ruined it.

Love, Pam

FLORENCE, ITALY - 31 January

With the Gulf War going on, I've decided to stay in Florence two extra days. I'll just pass through Frankfurt for a city tour, on my way to Hamburg. Frankfurt is such a military center right now, and there's so much to see in Florence. Even with the extra time, I'll have to come back.

I went to Piazzale Michelangelo today. It's on top of a big hill where the chic houses are located. From there you see Florence like it's a picture postcard.

While I was up there I called home from a pay phone at the Bar Ristorante la Loggia. It's the only place there is at Piazzale Michelangelo. After the phone call I had a lunch that was too expensive. Prosciutto, two slices of paper thin ham, bread, side salad, chocolate cake, and bottled water, I'd wanted tap, cost *$30.00US*. No dinner tonight.

Love, Pam

FLORENCE, ITALY - 31 January

I was writing postcards while sitting in the salon at Pensione Rigatti. I felt like I'd discovered the secret room of an old Renaissance palace. The room is not heated in winter, and it is scantily lit, but it has a huge antique dining table, that sits twelve, and a beautiful fresco on the ceiling.

As I sat admiring the room, my silence was disturbed when a woman came in saying "*buona sera*," good evening. I said "*buona sera*," then told her that that was the extent of my Italian. Hers too. We talked and she said the woman traveling with her was sick, and was worried about the luggage they had left checked at the train station. They'd taken a taxi from the train station and she didn't know how to get back. I did the neighborly thing and showed her how to get to the train station on the bus.

Love, Pam

FLORENCE, ITALY - 31 January

As I helped the woman, Carol, get the luggage from the train station, we traded bad back stories. With both of us working, the luggage wasn't heavy. Especially when the luggage guy at the train station puts it directly on the cart and the taxi driver puts it in the cab, and the doorman takes it to the room.

Carol is traveling with a black girl named Pam, who also has a *Round The World* ticket. Pam's great grandmother's maiden name is the same as our grandmother's from Alabama.

Small world, isn't it.

Love, Pam

FLORENCE, ITALY - 31 January

After getting the luggage, Carol and I went out looking for a cheap place to eat. In "Lets Go," there was a place nearby with a good antipasto plate, but they said we had to have a complete, a la carte, four course meal, so we went somewhere else.

I had spent too much money on lunch at Piazzale Michelangelo, so I wasn't going to eat anyway.

We found another place, the menu wasn't bad, but, there was too much linen and silverware on the table, for me to believe it would be a cheap place. Carol ordered hors d'oeuvres for me to split, and gave me some of her meat, the best steak I've ever tasted in my life. She treated, it was *$64.00US*. So much for cheap.

Love, Pam

FLORENCE, ITALY - 31 January

I feel very safe walking around Florence at night. I don't feel safe in Rome, even during the day. That's why I'd never go there alone.

Pam preferred Rome because it's more lively. Florence is more refined, even the tourist books say there's no night life in Florence.

Love, Pam

FLORENCE, ITALY - 1 February

For some reason, the owner at Pensione Rigatti assigned people a table to sit at breakfast, for the duration of their stay. No matter what, the housekeeper wasn't going to let you sit anywhere else. Until now a couple from Australia was seated next to me, but they departed yesterday. I was going to sit down with Pam

154.

and Carol, but that housekeeper would not hear of it, so I had to sit across the room, alone. The woman speaks no English, and *grazie*, and *buon giorno*, are the only other Italian words I know, so I couldn't reason with her.

Love, Pam

FLORENCE, ITALY - 1 February

I went to the Michelangelo house today, Casa Buonarroti, and saw some of his earlier works. You could see the progression. I really like this one stucco relief, *The Descention of Jesus from the Cross*. I didn't know Michelangelo worked in stucco. It is small, maybe 11x14 inches, and very detailed. It shows a mass of men with ladders and outstretched arms taking the body of Jesus down from the cross.

Before I went to the Michelangelo house, I went to the Bargello National Gallery. After I paid I saw the sign saying the Michelangelo room was closed. I almost cried.

It somewhat ruined my visit to that museum, until I saw the bronze baptistery panels of Brunelleschi, and Lorenzo Ghiberti. These were the panels from the contest for which artist got to do the Baptistery doors. The original Baptistery panels are at the Duomo museum.

Love, Pam

FLORENCE, ITALY - 1 February

The anti-war protesters in Florence also believe we are headed towards WWIII. It's weird not having any information. One woman protester couldn't believe that our pensione didn't have a satellite feed with CNN or anything English.

I met my first Kurd today in the tent. He's an art student. Carol had him draw her picture on Ponte Vecchio today. His family is still in Iraq. He's studying in Florence and doesn't want to go home. I've heard about the Kurds' situation but I didn't know what to say to him.

Love, Pam

FLORENCE, ITALY - 1 February

I took a half day tour today. With so many museums closed in the afternoon, in the winter, an afternoon tour made sense. We went to the Uffizi Gallery, and

Beatrice, our guide, explained the major pictures very well.

I thought the restoration of the only easel painting by Michelangelo, *Doni Tondo*, Holy family, was too cartoony. I did like the Botticellis, especially the *Birth of Venus*, as well as the Raphaels, da Vinci and others. We went to the Etruscan town, Fiesole, for 15 minutes.

All and all the tour was good, but not worth *$39.00US*. So I didn't tip her. I can't tip everyone.

Love, Pam

FLORENCE, ITALY - 1 February

The last time I came to Florence, it was with a tour group, for one afternoon. Our tour guide walked us through Florence and I wondered why she was taking us through back alleys. But that is Florence. Very narrow streets with trash dumpsters at either end which makes you think of American alley ways. Walking here does not have the same thrill as Paris or Vienna, but here there's such a sense of great history from these streets walked by Michelangelo, Dante, Donatello, Pisano, all the architects of the Renaissance.

Love, Pam

FLORENCE, ITALY - 2 February

The museums in Florence really know how to protect their art treasures. They all have temperature gauges, and at the Museo dell' Opera del Duomo, the original panels for the *gates of paradise*, from the Baptistery door, are sealed and weighted. Talk about museum quality. They also hang and present their art here better than they do at the Louvre in Paris. A lot of works are on the walls, but they compliment each other.

Love, Pam

FLORENCE, ITALY - 2 February

It was a beautiful sunny day today, and I decided to walk along the Arno across the Ponte Vecchio to the Pitti Palace. I took my tripod along and took pictures of myself as I walked. People always think it's strange when I do this, but if they traveled alone, they would realize it's a very good idea.

On my way, I stopped at the American Express Office to exchange money. That is where the Gulf War finally became a reality to me. I thought they were just opening, but they were unlocking the door for me to enter. Then they searched me with a metal detector. Wow!

See Card #2

Love, Pam

158.

FLORENCE, ITALY - 2 February

CARD #2

When the guard at the American Express office searched me with his electronic wand it started to beep next to my left hip. He assumed that's where my money belt was and that it set the beep off on the wand. My money belt was on the right side, but I didn't say anything. I have no idea what set off that wand.

Love, Pam

FLORENCE, ITALY - 3 February

Hi Mike,

All is well, but I'm cold. I got my room with a view in Florence. I also got a board for my bed so I'm happy. I've been museum hopping and trying to walk around, but the cobbles are really hurting my knee.

Did I write you before that teenagers in Austria really like the Raiders. They wore those expensive heavy wool Raider jackets, so I guess those exhibition games are beginning to pay off for Al Davis. Isn't that the Raiders owner? Oh well.

Love, Pam

FLORENCE, ITALY - 3 February

Yesterday, after the Pitti Palace I went over to the Medici Church. I thought there was a Michelangelo sculpture inside, but instead he designed the New Sacristy, and the Biblioteca Laurenzian, library entrance. There's no charge to enter the library. It's supposed to have a striking flight of stairs resembling a lava flow, but I could never find the library entrance. To see the *Dawn* and *Dusk, Night* and *Day* sculptures, you had to pay 85,000 lira, that's about *$8.50US*, to enter the Medici Chapel. I was too cheap.

Today is Sunday and everything is closed, except the Medici Chapel. I had hours to kill before the train, so I paid and saw it.

There were some US Art History students on a tour with their professor. So I listened in. It was very interesting. I don't think the professor liked me hanging around, but it's a public place, so tough.

Love, Pam

FLORENCE, ITALY - 3 February

After the Medici Chapel the only other place I could see was the *gates of paradise*, at least the copies that are on the Baptistery doors. Even though they did cast the moldings from the original doors, just as the copies of *David* look pale against the original in the Accademia Gallery, the *gates of paradise* looked dull compared to the original panels I saw on the Duomo Museum.

Love, Pam

FLORENCE, ITALY - 3 February

I'm glad I stayed the extra day in Florence, because today I got mail.

When I returned to Pensione Rigatti the proprietress presented me with a letter from my friend Sheila. It must have arrived yesterday. Sheila is apartment sitting for me while I travel. She's been around the world before and knew I would appreciate a letter from home. It never occurred to me that people could write me.

I'm glad I hadn't left town.

Love, Pam

FLORENCE, ITALY - 3 February

This is my last day in Florence. To save money, I'm catching an overnight train to Frankfurt, but I have to kill a lot of time until 6:00pm. It's a dreary day. It was drizzling earlier, then it stopped, but stayed cloudy. For a little while there were snow flurries. This is the second city I've been in where it tried to snow. The day I left Vienna was the other one. I think it's time to move on.

Love, Pam

FLORENCE, ITALY - 4 February

My last afternoon at the Pensione Rigatti reminded me of *A Room with a View*. Since it was cold and damp out, all of us with a late train ended up in the pensione day room for about six hours. Ed and his wife, from Seattle, married many years, and Wolfgang and his wife from Koln married one week. We talked the afternoon away, jumping from topic to topic. It was very relaxing.

Love, Pam

FLORENCE, ITALY - 4 February

To get to the train station, I had planned to take the bus. I didn't want to walk carting my things around in the dark and rain. I didn't have enough lira for a cab. Ed suggested calling the mini-van that had brought him and his wife to Pensione Rigatti. It was a great idea. Both couples and I took the mini-van for *$3.00US* each. A taxi cost *$9.00US*.

We stayed together at the train station until it was time to board.

Love, Pam

FLORENCE, ITALY - 4 February

It happened that we were all taking the same train at 8:44pm. It's very interesting about trains, we were all starting out on the same train but we were all going to different places. One couple to Koln, the other to Amsterdam and me to Frankfurt.

The train is broken apart en route, so it's important to get on the correct car for your destination.

Love, Pam

FRANKFURT, GERMANY - 4 February

European General Transit Card:

One of the main problems with the European Transit System is that if you don't have a ticket you can still board the transit. I did it in Venice to catch an early train. The Vaporetto ticket window wasn't open yet, so I took it free. If you get on with confidence, nobody knows.

I told this to Carol in Florence, and they never bought a bus ticket. When I asked Pam about a bus ticket she didn't even know what I was talking about. In theory they can do surprise checks and ask to see tickets. If you don't have a validated ticket you get fined.

Florence's fine is *$10.00US*, a one day ticket is *$4.00US*. I know checks happen but I've never seen it in action.

Love, Pam

FRANKFURT, GERMANY - 4 February

EUROPE GENERAL CARD:

All over Europe they seem to ride the transit system using the honor system. You can't even buy a ticket on the bus, tram, or subway. You have to buy them at tobacco shops or machines before hand. The transit system let's people enter through any door and they trust them to punch the ticket in the little box to validate it themselves. You don't have to validate it every time you board. You can buy a one day and multi-day pass, so most of the people board without punching anything. The assumption is they validated their ticket before. Ha!

Love, Pam

15

The great bank tour

FRANKFURT TRAIN STATION:

The twelve hour ride to Frankfurt was harder than the one to Venice. They didn't have a first class car that wasn't a sleeper, and the sleeper was full. I wound up in the second class seat compartment. Fortunately, I did find the no smoking car, but when I got on, Southern Italians, the train had come up from Rome, were inside hanging out the windows and smoking. There wasn't an empty compartment so when I went into one with a young man, about 20, who was smoking out the window. I said, to myself, but loud enough for him to hear, "I thought this was a no smoking car." Then I casually pointed to the no smoking symbol on the door, put my stuff down, and left to get my luggage. When I got back, he had moved out. I knew he would. Twelve hours of no smoking is impossible for the Europeans.

Love, Pam

FRANKFURT, GERMANY - 4 February

TRAIN STATION:

I arrived in Frankfurt, which is the only part of my trip I've changed so far because of the Gulf War.

I was supposed to spend the night, but instead I stayed in Florence a day and a half longer, and took an overnight train to Frankfurt to save the hotel money. Now I'm trying to get a city tour. Then I'll take the 2:33pm train to Hamburg. I may leave earlier, because if five people don't sign up for the tour, it won't take place. Only two of us have signed up so far, and there is only an hour before it starts.

I made the tour lady reissue my ticket and give me a refund when I saw the students 50% off discount sign, after I left the ticket counter. She gave me a mean look, and did not appreciate having to refund the money, but she did it anyway.

Good thing I signed up for a class and got a student card the semester before this trip. Even at almost thirty I can still be considered a student.

I thought I was going to be at the Frankfurt train station in the airport, which is a really great station with fancy boutiques, great for shopping. Instead I'm at the main station, it's cavernous and cold, and I have no idea where I am.

Love, Pam

FRANKFURT, GERMANY - 4 February

I had my Frankfurt City Tour today. Three people signed up at the last moment. I'm glad I stayed in Florence an extra day instead of staying in Frankfurt. Frankfurt is a rather charmless city, especially by European standards. It's really only 45 years old, because it was leveled at the end of World War II.

When a city tour keeps pointing out all the major banks in town, with pride, you know you have a problem. In addition to looking at banks, we went up the radio tower, for a view of the American military base, and we had a tour of the reconstructed Goethehaus.

Love, Pam

FRANKFURT, GERMANY - 4 February

I came back to the train station after the city tour. I got my things out of the locker, where three pickpockets, teenagers, were standing. They were talking, in English, about the police sweep at another train station the day before. I held onto my wallet.

I was hungry for something hearty, but not for a wurst. A young girl passed me with a wonderful smelling meat filled bread that looked like a gyro. She didn't speak English, but I found the gyro stand. It was very good. I had it with apfelstaf, German apple cider, I love that stuff.

Love, Pam

16

I didn't tip him...
I should have

I arrived in Hamburg at night. It's the only city I've arrived in after dark. I found the hotel that I had arranged to stay at from the states. When I arrived, there was just one other man there sitting in the lobby. He kind of gave me the creeps.

I made my first mistake when I said, "Hello." I thought he was the proprietor, he wasn't. The proprietor was sitting in the dark behind the desk. I checked in, got my key and proceeded to my room. The man in the lobby followed me to my room and stood in the doorway so I couldn't close the door. He started asking me if I was married, and where my husband was. Since I had a room where I had to go out of into the hallway to use the restroom, I didn't feel comfortable. Especially since I felt that this man and I were the only people in the entire hotel. See Card #2

Love, Pam

HAMBURG, GERMANY - 4 February

CARD #2

I waited a minute after the man left, gathered my things and told the man at the front desk that I didn't feel comfortable staying at his hotel. Fortunately I hadn't paid for the room. I went out into the Hamburg night and back to the Hauptbahnhof train station, to the tourist desk. They gave me the name of two hotels nearby. The first one was more expensive than the tourist office said, so I rejected it and went to the second one. They were full, but told me to try next door. I did, and they had a room, so I ended up at the Hotel Aachner.

The front desk people were very nice. The room had a shower in it, and the desk man brought me an extra blanket because it was very cold.

They served a very substantial breakfast the next morning, German breads and cold cuts.

Love, Pam

HAMBURG, GERMANY - 5 February

I got up this morning, and it was snowing a little bit, but worse, it was very icy out. All I wanted to do was get through the day without falling. On my way to the Steinway piano factory, I got to the Metro station, took the subway, and exited the subway station to catch the bus. I determined where to go to catch the bus, started across the street and fell. Hard. Three people came to my aid. I stood up, brushed myself off, they left, I took one step and fell again. This time a man and an older woman helped me. The woman put a vice grip on my arm and led me to the bus stop. I'm leaving Hamburg tomorrow.

Love, Pam

HAMBURG, GERMANY - 5 February

After falling on the ice, I got the bus for Steinway, I asked the bus driver to call the street. He appeared to understand what I was saying. When he got to the street, it was a street that the bus stays on for some time. He couldn't tell me where to get off. There were no visible addresses in the area, so I stayed on for one more stop. Of course, as soon as the bus pulled away, I saw the Steinway sign.

I had to walk back, up hill, praying that I wouldn't fall again.

I got to Steinway and had to wait awhile for Mr. Kalb. He was very kind and generous. He arranged for an apprentice to take me around, and a free taxi ride back to the hotel.

Love, Pam

HAMBURG, GERMANY - 5 February

I had a great tour of the Hamburg Steinway factory. The apprentice took me through each stage of production from wood bending to finished product. He is in a 3½ year program, after which he is guaranteed employment with Steinway for life.

They have a kind of fraternity there, you can tell by the looks and expressions that pass between the craftsmen. All the men were very kind to the apprentice. Only four women work at the factory and there is only one woman apprentice.

It was an interesting and informative tour.

Love, Pam

HAMBURG, GERMANY - 5 February

It takes two and a half years to make a Steinway piano, any piano, upright or concert grand. It is tuned and voiced seven times. I was allowed to take pictures everywhere except the soundboard building area. That is the secret to all piano factories. Apparently, two Japanese men came through one day, one asking questions, the other taking pictures, non-stop, so the plant supervisor prohibits pictures in this area anymore. Evidently, once the piano is put together and lacquered, you can't see the sound board detail as well anymore.

Love, Pam

HAMBURG, GERMANY - 5 February

To get the mirror finish on a Steinway piano takes one week per instrument. They sand and polish them seven times. This is the hardest thing for an apprentice to learn. It can take one year for an apprentice to learn to do it so that it is acceptable to ship.

Talk about shipping. When we got to the last room, the shipping room, they were moving a piano and they almost dropped it. two and a half years of work almost ruined.

Love, Pam

HAMBURG, GERMANY - 5 February

There are seven woods used in making the Steinway Piano. The wood used for primary sound is spruce, followed by a very hard wood called metal to stabilize it. All the layers are glued together so they bond as one in a piano shaped press for 72 hours.

They sand the part of the soundboard that holds the strings, with water and emery paper. I saw the product as, it started out very rough, and it ended very very smooth, like satin.

The keys must be exact when they are put in position. They have a one millimeter margin for error.

I tipped the apprentice 10 Deutsche marks, *$8.00US,* for the tour. They get paid very little. He appreciated it. The tour didn't cost me anything, and he did an excellent job. I took his picture by a piano and he took mine next to one.

Love, Pam

HAMBURG, GERMANY - 5 February

The taxi driver who picked me up from Steinway spoke English and because I was in so much pain after the falls, I paid him 40 Deutsche marks, *$28.00US* to give me a city tour. First I had to get money at a bank, which took forever to exchange. Of course my taxi meter was running.

The tour was good, as good as possible with the snow. He took me in a car elevator and into the Alte Elbe-Tunnel, across the Elbe River. It is a one fourth mile tunnel under the Elbe, built in 1911. It cost 2 Deutsche marks, each direction, but he was very savvy and made a U-turn at the end so we didn't have to pay to return.

I was cheap and didn't tip him. I should have.

Love, Pam

HAMBURG, GERMANY - 6 February

It snowed again last night, so I left Hamburg a day early. It hadn't snowed for five years in Hamburg, until I showed up. I didn't like the Hamburg Hauptbahnhof train station, there appeared to be too many transients. I may be wrong, but I kept thinking someone was trying to pick my pocket. I know it's cultural, but everyone stood too close in line when they didn't have to.

Also, at Hauptbahnhof, the train station, you have to go down a very long flight of stairs to get to the train. There are no elevators or escalators for going down, only up. I had to lug my luggage down a long flight of stairs with a very sore back.

They had no waiting area, and no heat. It was freezing.

I got kicked out of my seat in Hanover, because I didn't have a reservation, just a Eurailpass. I had to sit in the second class car to Munich.

Love, Pam

MUNICH, GERMANY - 6 February

I went to the waiting room in the Hauptbahnhof train station in Munich, grateful they had one, unlike Hamburg. Even better, it was nonsmoking. It was fairly full with travelers but I found a seat next to a quiet drunk. I was reading the paper when all of a sudden one drunk in the room started singing opera. We all snickered. The other drunks told him to shut up. Then the train guard came in and threw out everyone who didin't have a ticket. Some of the drunks tried to argue, but they lost.

Love, Pam

MUNICH, GOING TO BERLIN, GERMANY - 6 February

I saw this postcard of earth from space with Munich marked on it in the

Munich Hauptbahnhof train station. I thought it would be appropriate with my around the world trip, a sort of "Where am I now?" Munich has a lovely train station. They have a bakery that makes great bread. The train ride into Munich was good until Hanover when all these people got on the train with reservations and I had to move to second class. It didn't say that train needed a reservation in the Eurail book.

Second class was fine though, the seats were actually better for my back, but you could smell the smokers. I took the time to sew the pocket on my heavy coat and reinforce a couple of the buttons. I know it's stupid to be going down to Munich from Hamburg and then up to Berlin but I wanted to save the money on a day's lodging.

Love, Pam

17

What is Nefertiti doing in Berlin?

BERLIN, GERMANY - 7 February

I arrived at 7:30 in the morning and got a city tour at 10:00am, that included both East and West Berlin. It was interesting, our Greek guide told us when we were going from one side to the other. They really have torn down that big wall. If you look hard, you can find some sections but you have to be looking for them. The first few times she pointed it out, I couldn't even find it. It was really weird knowing that it once surrounded the city, and now you can hardly find it.

Love, Pam

BERLIN, GERMANY - 7 February

I'm in Berlin, I really knew it when I saw pieces of what's left of the wall. I had a man take pictures of me near it, I hope they come out.

I couldn't get close enough to touch it because there was too much ice from the snow, and I wasn't going to risk falling again. But I was close, and I was there.

Love, Pam

BERLIN, GERMANY - 7 February

A couple on the half-day tour in Florence told me not to miss the Pergamon Museum in East Berlin. I had never even heard of it before. They were right, it is quite a museum. I saw it on my Berlin tour. The tour company was great in that they included in the price the cassette tape tour of the museum so everyone could hear it in their own language.

They have reconstructed an ancient Greek altar, the actual *Pergamon altar*, in the museum as well as the *Market Gate at Miletus*, and mosaic walls from the *Babylonian Processional Way*. It's really something to see. Most fascinating is the frieze surrounding the altar, depicting the struggle of the Greek gods against

181.

the giants. The altar was originally destroyed and used to build part of the city wall. It was discovered thousands of years later, excavated, and reassembled back in Berlin. It's considered to be almost the eighth wonder of the ancient world.

Love, Pam

BERLIN, GERMANY - 7 February

I went into the Egyptian Museum almost out of a courtesy to the past, to see the famous bust of *Nefertiti*. My eighth grade history teacher, Mr. Woods, had raved about its beauty. I thought he was just reading from books.

This bust is the shining star of a magnificent museum. I first saw the bust from down stairs. The lighting on it is so effective, it just makes you want to see it. I had no idea it existed in Berlin. It was brought to Berlin as the German half of an archaeological find in Egypt. The tour brought us here. If I was staying another day, I'd return here. But Berlin is colder than Hamburg.

Love, Pam

BERLIN, GERMANY - 7 February

Mr. Woods used to go on and on about *Nefertiti* and her great beauty. He said a bust had been made of her as an example of what the most beautiful woman looked like. I never thought much about the picture in the history book, but today I saw the original. Pictures do not do justice to this beautiful bust.

Love, Pam

BERLIN, GERMANY - 7 February

My first view of Berlin was complete with Burger King and McDonald's, as well as the Kaiser-Wilhelm-Gedachtniskirche, Kaiser-Wilhem-Memorial Church Tower.

The shell of the church tower is what remains of a church built in the 19th Century and dedicated to the memory of Kaiser-Wilhelm. It was destroyed in World War II bombings. It now houses a museum and there are ten minute church services there every day. I had wanted to go to services there, but I couldn't figure out what time they started.

I don't know if I mentioned it, but, in Florence, I never saw McDonald's or Wendy's or any American fast food place. There were three McDonald's inside the Ring, in Vienna. I know, I ate at Mickey-D's three times in Vienna, but none since. Right after India, remember? I wanted meat, even cheap meat. At least I knew the meat wasn't mutton.

I liked Berlin, but I would have liked to visit it, and Hamburg, in the spring or fall. Berlin does a terrific job of snow maintenance, lots of sand and plowing, but the bitter cold against my L.A. skin is making me leave early.

Love, Pam

BERLIN, GERMANY - 7 February

After the tour of Berlin, I made my way back to the Brandenburg Gate. The tour went by it but didn't stop. I went over to a food vendor and asked an older woman if she would take my picture. She didn't speak English, but she understood. She thought it was amusing, but she took it. I was wearing the green bomber hat, I looked stupid, but who cares when you're cold. That was one picture I really wanted on this trip. I'm glad I got it.

I couldn't find my way back to the Checkpoint Charlie Museum, too bad, I'll see it next time.

Love, Pam

BERLIN, GERMANY - 7 February

My hotel is apparently somewhere near the palace Schloß Charlottenburg, here in the Charlottenburger district. We passed the palace on the city tour but I didn't see my hotel. I know my hotel's right by a S-Bahn, above ground subway station, you can hear the trains. The Hotel Charlottenburger Hof is just okay. I am surprised since it was starred in Frommer's. The beds are cots like Venice, but sleepable, for one night, because they are newer. The chairs are cheap plastic stack chairs, but thankfully they have lots of heat.

Love, Pam

BERLIN, GERMANY - 7 February

One of the interesting facts I found out, from the man at the hotel desk, about the wall coming down, was that East Berlin never destroyed or damaged its train and subway tracks that lead to West Berlin. Which means when the wall came down the trains could just drive through. Even the train stations had remained unused since 1961. I had wondered how they had built so much in one year. Especially considering how long it takes L.A. to build one mile of its Metro.

Love, Pam

BERLIN, GERMANY - 7 February
THIS IS A GENERAL EUROPE CARD:

Without fail, every hotel I have stayed in so far, which asked me to send money before hand, failed to acknowledge it when I arrived. In Venice and Berlin I had to offer to show them a copy of the draft. This was enough to jerk their memories.

In Florence, I knew she got the check because she gave me the room I requested, but I still had to remind her when she filled out the bill in full. Let's be honest.

Love, Pam

BERLIN, GERMANY - 7 February

I've seen a lot of Germany in a few days. The cities I didn't stay in I passed through on the train. I went to Frankfurt, Hamburg, Munich and Berlin. The overall common characteristic is that they're all cold, especially Berlin where it is bone-biting.

The service people in Berlin all seem to be in a bad mood. Or maybe it's the German language and way of talking. The hotel people have all been very nice, but none of them are willing to drop their rates.

Love, Pam

BERLIN, GERMANY - 7 February

Because of my short stint, and because of the weather, I have not been able to get an attitude on the German people one year after the wall.

Before getting to Berlin, I heard there was a running joke to put the wall back and build it two meters higher. Also that you could buy T-shirts with 2M, for two meters higher. But I haven't seen any. To be honest, I haven't seen any T-shirts whatsoever, it's just too cold.

Love, Pam

18

Running away from the cold

MUNICH, BERLIN, MUNICH, GERMANY - 8 February

Two days ago I took the train from Hamburg to Munich hoping to get out of the snow. It was like going from Northern California to San Diego. As we entered Munich I could see it had snowed here as well. So I went to Berlin. At least there the roads had a lot of sand.

Now I've decided to go to Nice, expecting rain. Except sitting in the train station in Munich again, "USA Today" says snow flurries for Nice. Maybe that means it won't stick. We will see.

Oh yeah, I just found out, it's Carnival in Nice, so finding a hotel will be nearly impossible. Wish me luck.

Love, Pam

MUNICH, GERMANY - 8 February

9:00pm approximately - what a trip.

As I was waiting in the waiting room among the travelers and drunks in Munich's Hauptbahnhof train station, the guard came in and in German told everyone to leave. I wasn't sure he initially meant everyone, because when the guard came in the other night, he kicked out everyone without a ticket. A young person outside later translated to me that there is a bomb threat in the luggage lockers next to the room. Apparently, this is the second bomb threat this week.

Love, Pam

MUNICH, GERMANY - 8 February

I'm not really sure if there was a bomb threat at the train station, it's not as if the station was cleared or even the area. They made us leave the waiting room and wait in the cold right outside the waiting room for over an hour. You'd think if there was a true threat they would have made us move far away. They did let the custodian in to clean during this time. The problem is without the waiting area, there's no place to sit in the entire train station. It's their way of keeping the homeless out.

Oh, a French guy I met waiting in the cold said there was snow in Nice.

Love, Pam

MILAN, ITALY - 10 February

I took the overnight train from Munich to Milan. They sure give the Italians the older, worn down trains. It seemed to take forever. I was looking to get out of the snow, as well as see the *Last Supper* and the *Duomo*. As the train got further south, the snow stayed just as thick. I'd have even gone for heavy rain.

As the trip progressed I realized I had to end my trip, it wasn't fun anymore with the snow and ice. I called home from the Milan Centrale train station and headed for Zürich.

Love, Pam

ZÜRICH, SWITZERLAND - 10 February

On my way to Zürich, the weather gave me hope at times because the mountains and valleys were green in some areas. I decided to fly to Paris on SwissAir and fly Delta home, if mom wasn't worried about me flying a US carrier overseas. Of course, when the train got to Zürich there was snow everywhere. The Paris hotel was full, so I checked into the Novotel, because I'd used them in Cannes once before on a bus tour, and more important was because they had free airport transportation.

Love, Pam

ZÜRICH, SWITZERLAND - 10 February

I met an American couple living in Germany during dinner at the Novotel. He had worked for the Peace Corps several years ago and then gone on a *Round The World* trip. She wanted to know if I'd do it again. He looked at me and smiled slightly, knowing that I'd do it again in a minute, after I had some rest. It was then that I realized that there is this kind of RTW club between people that have taken this type of trip. It's unspoken but there is a connection with all of us because so few people do it.

Love, Pam

ZÜRICH, SWITZERLAND - 10 February

The Novotel is wonderful, a real hotel room. I took a long tub bath until my fingers shriveled.
The Fielding's, "Budget Asia" book was right, a night in a good hotel does wonders for a person's state of mind. A full size bed, an attached bath, and cable TV, life is good.

Love, Pam

19

There's a backpack they must speak English

PARIS, FRANCE - 11 February

When I arrived in Paris there was snow on the ground. I wanted to cry. As the RER, fast metro, got to the city from the airport, no snow. Just cold. Très bien.

Love, Pam

PARIS, FRANCE - 11 February

When I called Hôtel Esmeralda from the Zürich airport he said he had a tiny room available today and a larger room tomorrow. He certainly didn't lie. This room is very tiny, the bed barely fits, but they still forced a rickety table and chair in the room with it. The bathroom is ridiculously small. There's a mini sink, the toilet is squeezed into a narrow recessed space, and the shower is half the size of a small shower. There's a shower curtain because a shower door couldn't fit in the bathroom.

See Card #2

Love, Pam

PARIS, FRANCE - 11 February

CARD #2

The Frommer's guide book said many of the rooms at Hôtel Esmeralda have a view of Notre-Dame. This isn't one of them. My view is of a narrow outside storage area with buckets, brooms, and half-wilted potted plants. I'm directly across the street from Notre-Dame and you'd never know it.

Love, Pam

PARIS, FRANCE - 11 February

I arrived in Paris on Sunday, and I thought it would be great to go to mass at Notre-Dame. I went across the street and read the door, they had one evening mass. Great. The time was listed in military time, and there was an organ concert before hand, yuck. I had an hour to kill, so I walked among the book vendors on the Siene. Finally I looked at my watch. Not wanting to be late, I had 10 minutes to get to church, on aching legs. I finally flagged a taxi and he got me there with three minutes to spare, so I tipped him well.

Once inside, I found the organ concert continued and I realized I'd computed the 24 hours wrong, and had 45 minutes to wait. I left. Didn't this bring back memories of the opera in Vienna?

Love, Pam

PARIS, FRANCE - 11 February

I had a chicken of the day dinner at a non-descript nearby café. The chicken was a little pink but I didn't want the hassle involved trying to send it back so I ate it because I was hungry. An hour later my chicken dinner is all over the toilet in my tiny bathroom. I tried to clean it up but there just isn't enough room. I just feel too bad to try any harder. I'll use the common toilet down the hall until the maid cleans it up in the morning.
See Card #2

Love, Pam

PARIS, FRANCE - 12 February

CARD #2

The maid knocked and told me she had a new, larger room for me. I told her I vomited all over the toilet. Amazingly the word's the same in French as in English. I saw a not too pleased look on her face at the prospect of cleaning it up. I gave her 20 French francs, *$4.00US*, it appeased her. Good thing, it was all I had.

See Card #3

Love, Pam

PARIS, FRANCE - 12 February

CARD #3

My new room is big, almost huge. Not just compared to the tiny room but compared to most of the other rooms on my trip. It has a queen size bed, antique dressers, a sturdy writing table and chair, and red velvet bordello wallpaper. The bathroom is spacious, with a tub, normal size sink, and toilet well spread out over the room. My view is almost of Notre-Dame, if you look to the side, but I am across from a very pleasant, quaint, little park, with benches. I'm going to enjoy this.

Love, Pam

PARIS, FRANCE - 12 February

I took the Metro to see the Eiffel Tower and when I first exited there was a sign with an arrow pointing straight telling tourists to go 300 meters then turn at some bridge, so I walked straight. When I got to a stop light I didn't see a bridge, I happened to look behind me, and there the Eiffel Tower was. I'd walked the wrong way. I walked back to the Metro, re-read the sign, then read the sign on the other side. The other sign said 300 meters behind you. Someone had switched the sign to fool the tourists, and because of a tall wall, the parallax view doesn't let you see the Eiffel Tower from the Metro. I wasn't amused at the joke.

Love, Pam

PARIS, FRANCE - 12 February

After a rough morning, the sun came out and melted the snow so I decided to go to the Eiffel Tower. I bought an all day Metro ticket. I should have bought ten strips instead, they're cheaper. When I went to the Eiffel Tower I knew I wanted to go to the top but I hadn't changed any money yet. Wouldn't you know, the change kiosk was closed today, and there was a big sign saying, French francs only. It cost 49 French francs to go to the top, I had 48 ½ French francs. I couldn't believe it. Because the Eiffel Tower is here, there's nowhere else to go for change.

I listened for an American voice, but there were none. I saw two guys get off a tour bus with backpacks, I hoped they were American. They were British, but they had just been up and exchanged 4 French francs for 1 US dollar. I went to the top.

Love, Pam

PARIS, FRANCE - 12 February

Everyone is so excited when they get to the top of the Eiffel Tower. You can see all of Paris laid out like spokes on a wheel. The outdoor lookout area is fenced off, I guess because people have jumped. The second level is high enough to jump also but it's not fenced. I prefer the unobstructive view from the second level.

Love, Pam

PARIS, FRANCE - 12 February

It's cold at the top of the Eiffel Tower, which made most of us view the city from the inside room. I met two Indian guys from Singapore up here. Nice guys.

They saved money and walked the several hundred stairs up to the second level of the Eiffel Tower. You have to take the elevator to get to the third level. We chatted for a while about Singapore and India. They have family in Delhi. They are off to London next. We also spoke about Singapore airlines and how great they are, especially the Big Top 747's.

Love, Pam

PARIS, FRANCE - 12 February

When I got to the bottom of the Eiffel Tower I headed for the pillar where the famous Jules Verne restaurant is located. It's very expensive but I was only going to get a hot chocolate. I wanted to see what it looks like inside, and say I'd been there. I got to the door just as it was closing from lunch. I didn't realize I'd been up sightseeing for so long, but it was 2:00pm. The day's so gray you can't even feel the time change.

Love, Pam

PARIS, FRANCE - 13 February

I woke up feeling horrible and decided to use the American Express travel insurance Mom gave me as a gift, to call a doctor. I got the English speaking doctor number from my Frommer's, telling them I had American Express insurance. They told me no doctor takes the American Express card and I'd have to pay cash. CASH!!! For a house call, that would cost a fortune. She guaranteed me it would cost 100 French francs, *$20.00US*. That's it? I could afford 100 French francs.

See Card #2

Love, Pam

PARIS, FRANCE - 13 February

CARD #2

The doctor came, what a jerk, even if he did speak English. He listened to my chest, said I had bronchitis and wrote several prescriptions, after I told him all the antibiotics I was allergic to. I wanted him to look at my back because I could barely get out of bed. He watched me struggle to get up and stand straight, but he did nothing. He just made a call on his cellular phone and left me in pain. Jerk.

Love, Pam

PARIS, FRANCE - 13 February

I found a nearby pharmacy to fill my prescriptions. If socialized medicine makes a doctor's visit $20.00US I was expecting $5.00US for the prescriptions.

Wrong. The prescriptions cost as much as the doctor.

I forgot there are certain medicines you can get over the counter in Europe that you can only get by prescription in the states. When I asked for cough drops I was relieved I read the ingredients before I took one.

See Card #2

Love, Pam

PARIS, FRANCE - 13 February

CARD #2

I was half way home when I read the ingredients on the cough drops box. It had the French word for codeine, and I'm allergic to codeine. It was spelled too similar to the English word for codeine not to be codeine, and I wasn't going to take any chances. The pharmacist confirmed my suspicions and gave me something weaker.

Love, Pam

PARIS, FRANCE - 13 February

I finally got the postcard of the Notre-Dame rose window I wanted when the bus was leaving last June. Notre-Dame has the most beautiful stain glassed windows in the world and you can only get this particular card across the street from it. They dismantled and numbered the pieces of the windows during World War II so it wouldn't be destroyed.

Yes, I went out even after the doctor's visit. I couldn't stay in bed in Paris.

Right now I'm sick and leaving for home tomorrow morning.

Love, Pam

PARIS, FRANCE - 14 February

What a lousy morning. As I depart from Paris, I spent a fortune getting to the airport. First I took a cab to Aéroport Charles-de-Gaulle, he charged me 30 French francs, $7.00US, to pick me up. He charged from the moment he got the call. Then I got to Aéroport Charles-de-Gaulle, and realized Delta is at Orly Airport.

This cab driver drove slow so I wasn't about to have him drive me back. I took the Air France bus, which took forever to come, and my luggage cart broke in the rush to board the bus.

Love, Pam

PARIS, FRANCE - 14 February

LAST DAY AROUND THE WORLD TRIP:

I am ending my trip early due to illness, bronchitis, bad back, bad knees, and the worst weather in Europe in 94 years, according to the US newspapers. I'm glad I got to Paris before going home, it was a good ending to my trip.

Nothing, however, went right this last morning. It snowed, so I didn't get to Ash Wednesday mass at Notre-Dame. The taxi driver to Aéroport Charles-de-Gaulle drove slower than all the other taxis and cars. They were all passing him by. I didn't tip him. The change people took forever to exchange a Japanese lady's money. I didn't see a bathroom so I just reached my hand in my pants in front of everyone to get a Travelers Cheque to change for French francs to take the bus to Orly Airport. I stood outside in the cold as the Air France bus driver ran from place to place, instead of letting us wait on the bus. My last stamps fell in back of the bus seat, and I couldn't get them. Good-bye Paris.

Love, Pam

*PARIS, FRANCE TO ATLANTA, GEORGIA & LOS ANGELES, CALIFORNIA, USA
14 February*

I hope I remember to write Delta about the wonderful service on Flight 21,

February 14, 1991. It was even better than Singapore, because the flight crew was so kind and personable. It was also a pleasure hearing those wonderful American southern accents when I boarded the plane for home.

Love, Pam

In memory of Pensione Rigatti
I'll always remember my room with a view.

Order A Copy For A Friend

Around the World
A Postcard Adventure

Quest press P.O. Box 3653 Beverly Hills, CA 90212 USA
(800) 590-7778 • (213) 934-2881 fax • (213) 935-6666 outside USA
e-mail Questpress@aol.com

Send me _____ number of copies

I am enclosing _____ at $12.95 each ($14.95 Canada)

plus $3 shipping 1st book $1 each additional book/foreign orders $4US 1st, $2 each additional
(CA residents add 8.25% sales tax)

TOTAL $_____ Send check or money order - No cash or C.O.D. please

Method of payment:

    Check   VISA   Mastercard   (circle one)

Card# _____ exp. date _____

Name as appears on credit card _____

Signature _____

Telephone# _____

Mail to: (please print)
Name _____
Address _____
City/State _____ Zip _____

Call toll free and order now

Order A Copy For A Friend

Around the World
A Postcard Adventure

Quest press P.O. Box 3653 Beverly Hills, CA 90212 USA
(800) 590-7778 • (213) 934-2881 fax • (213) 935-6666 outside USA
e-mail Questpress@aol.com

Send me _____ number of copies

I am enclosing _____ at $12.95 each ($14.95 Canada)

plus $3 shipping 1st book $1 each additional book/foreign orders $4US 1st, $2 each additional
(CA residents add 8.25% sales tax)

TOTAL $_____ Send check or money order - No cash or C.O.D. please

Method of payment:

    Check   VISA   Mastercard (circle one)

Card# _____ exp. date _____

Name as appears on credit card _____

Signature _____

Telephone# _____

Mail to: (please print)

Name _____

Address _____

City/State _____, Zip _____

Call toll free and order now